MANHOOD

NAVIGATING THE MIND FIELDS

PETER O. PRITCHARD

Bridge-Logos
Alachua, Florida

Bridge-Logos
Alachua, FL 32615 USA

Manhood—Navigating the Mind Fields
by Peter O. Pritchard

Printed in the United States of America.

Library of Congress Catalog Card Number: 2008926144
International Standard Book Number 978-0-88270-479-1

Scripture quotations marked (KJV) are from the *King James* version of the Bible. Italics in Scripture quotations are those of the author to direct the reader's attention to the words emphasized.

G222.316.N.m806.35250

Introduction

Countless Christians read the "Proverb of the Day" as a daily devotional guide for each date of every month. As no month has more than thirty-one days and there are thirty-one chapters in the Book of Proverbs, it is easy to see how this devotional regimen has achieved both popularity and consistency among believers for many years.

The Book of Proverbs itself tells us in its very first passage (1:1-5) what its teachings are intended to produce in one's life. They are "for *attaining* wisdom and discipline; for *understanding* words of insight; for *acquiring* a disciplined and prudent life, *doing* what is right and just and fair" (verses 2-3).

Within the same passage is identification of just for *whom* these Proverbs are intended, for they are to instruct "the simple," "the young," and "the wise" (verses 4-5). Regarding the simple, we are told they shall be given "prudence," the very thing they lack—it is because of this deficiency they are obviously and rightly surmised as, well, *simple*. For the "young" (or perhaps as easily put, the *inexperienced*) they shall receive from the Proverbs what they have thus far been unable to proffer from life's experiences "knowledge" and "discretion." And for those few and fortunate enough to have become wise and discerning already coursing through this life, the Proverbs shall not be inconsequential for them whatsoever but shall "add to their learning" (verse 5).

For many years now I, too, have regularly read a Proverb each day of the twenty-eight to thirty-one days of the month (when I am faithful and conscientious enough to read God's Holy Word that particular day). So when I felt compelled to write a devotional book to inspire my fellow brothers in Christ to walk *along with me* as purely as possible before God and our covenants, I decided that a thirty-one-day devotional would be best.

First, a thirty-one-day devotional covers each day of every month of the year. Yet, unlike a 365-day devotional, it pays closer attention to the *realism* that some days will more than likely be missed with some regularity. When that occurs, its corollary devotional shall in most cases be read the very next month, versus having no opportunity for reflection upon that particular devotional for another whole year.

Second, it is perhaps most helpful and effectual when a godly man is encouraged, admonished, inspired, and strengthened by these inspirations once a month versus only once a year as in 365-day devotionals.

And, lastly, because this devotional (in contrast to most daily devotionals) has but one single, solitary aim—mental moral purity for men—it is believed this theme in particular resonates well with the prior stated objective of the original Proverbs: that they are "for attaining *wisdom* and *discipline.*"

This point is so essential to the intent of the original Proverbs—to God, its true Author—it is *restated* (in only slightly different manner) immediately in verse 3:

these meditations are "for acquiring a *disciplined* and *prudent* life."

In the area of male mental moral purity, there are no two character traits more important and more mandatory for victorious living than attaining wisdom and discipline. *Wisdom* is acquiring insight into ourselves and understanding the tempter, discerning the temptations, our options, the opportunities, and the *consequences* to indulgence. *Discipline* is teaching us and instilling us with *self-control* (the final of the nine attributes of the Fruit of the Spirit (Galatians 5:21), which is synonymous with living a disciplined life.

We are barely into the new millennium, and it is common knowledge within the Church that our times are fraught with spiritual potholes, moral land mines, and insidious cultural ambushes like never before. These are decidedly aimed at undermining male mental moral purity, tripping us up, Brothers, and if possible destroying the man of God.

For decades the impurity on television and in movies has promulgated its wares basically unchallenged and unabated. However, the newest innovation and single most potent implement that the devil has ever had at his disposal is undeniably the Internet. What makes the Internet most useful to Satan in this regard is that:

1) It has little to no censorship;

2) It is very inexpensive;

3) It offers instantaneous gratification; and,

4) It offers a *false* sense of seclusion, privacy, and anonymity (perhaps its greatest advantage to our adversary the devil).

The Internet in and of itself, of course, is *amoral*; it is merely a medium of communication that is neither good nor bad. When critiqued solely for its technological ingenuity, it is a modern-day marvel and a blessing in regard to all of the good and helpful information it can relay. Its global content offerings and efficiencies in respect to the news, academic learning, business commerce, military defense, law enforcement, and innumerable and assorted other correspondents and *correspondence*—not to mention the e-mail support it provides linking us with our distant loved ones, missionaries, and soldiers—make it of unquestionable benefit. In immeasurable ways, the Internet has truly become invaluable.

Yet, it is a tool with cataclysmic implications. Just as such a completely benign and unsophisticated tool as a hammer can be used to build a church or crack a skull, the Internet has become a tool of great good while simultaneously becoming a tool of devastatingly destructive capabilities when deployed at the whims and wiles of Satan. And he must be ecstatic that it is so readily accessible to human hearts insubmissive to the knowledge, will, and power of God.

Matthew 16:18 implies that the Church is to be on the *offensive*—that the very "gates of hell shall not prevail against it" (KJV). Much of this thirty-one-day devotional is an unabashed, direct, and frontal counterattack to Satan's cunning exploitation of lives through the lies and lures of the Internet.

Proverbs 27:20 describes the roving eyes of a man in this alarming way: "Death and Destruction are never satisfied, and neither are the eyes of man." Solomon is exposing the universal weakness of our eyes—more accurately put, the desires of our hearts only aided through our eyes—as having an insatiable appetite and being "never satisfied." This proverb is no mere exposé on our male propensity alone but a chilling warning as to what the unchecked, unbridled eyes of the male will lead to—death and destruction!

God is not against sexual pleasure. After all, He's the One who came up with the idea. [Read Proverbs 5:18-19 and tell me God is against sexual fun.] He devised sexuality and made the material and moral provisions for it. God not only created sex for the utilitarian purposes of procreation but for the purposes of providing us with the ultimate in marital intimacy, ultimate satisfaction, and supreme enjoyment in the holy context of marriage.

Satan, on the other hand, is the great counterfeiter. The devil is a master deceiver, in truth "the father of lies" (John 8:44). Through pornography, he offers men *virtual* sexual satisfaction in exchange for what God offers us—*virtuous* sexual fulfillment. As Christ's disciples—His precious sought, bought, and taught men of God—we must stand our ground and where necessary, Brothers, regain and keep our ground, choosing virtuous sexual fulfillment over virtual sexual satisfaction here, now, and forevermore!

Likeminded with the Apostle Paul's anguished lament of Romans 7, many of us men do not do what we want to do and inexplicably do what we *do not want to do.* This thirty-one-day devotional is a primer intended to change that condition in the area of male mental moral purity—to "restore him gently" (Galatians 6:1), to "carry each other's burdens"(Galatians 6:2), to turn the ship around in the lives of good men who in some cases we must literally "snatch ... from the fire and save them" (Jude 1:23).

In my own life—as one who has experienced some measure of personal failure in these areas before—the Holy

Spirit has reminded me of Jesus' affirming words to Simon Peter shortly before Peter failed his Lord: "And when you have turned back, strengthen your brothers" (Luke 22:32). Here I am to strengthen you, Brothers. You should also know that *I believe in you* (see Romans 15:14).

May these thirty-one devotionals reinspire us, reignite the passion, rejuvenate Christ's deposited wisdom and strength, and reinvigorate us to follow God and His commandments in the way we genuinely *want to do* and are *enabled to do* by the power of His Spirit within us (see 1 Corinthians 1:8, 2 Peter 1:3, Romans 14:4b).

In 2 Timothy 2:22, the Apostle Paul admonished his dear and faithful protégé Timothy, as well as the church over which Timothy was overseer, and now us, their spiritual descendants: "Flee the evil desires of youth, and pursue righteousness, faith, love and peace, along with those who call on the Lord out of a pure heart." (If you are allowed to write in your Bible, by all means underline, highlight, or circle "along with.")

Let's embark on this journey *along with* one another, Brothers! Let's together become men well-known in matters of purity for our scriptural integrity and spiritual valor. "As iron sharpens iron, so one man sharpens another" (Proverbs 27:17). Let us "encourage one another daily" (Hebrews 3:13), united to the finish line (Acts 20:24, 2 Timothy 4:7), finishing as well as we started with as few stragglers and fewer casualties along the way as possible. Let us, Brothers, "flee the evil desires of youth, and pursue righteousness, faith, love and peace" *together*, calling upon our God and His strength "out of a pure heart."

The questions at the end of each day are designed to help you understand the insights of this book more clearly and to apply them to your life. They may be used by either individuals or groups. May God bless you richly as you delve more deeply into the important, practical subject matter of this book.

1. What is the "single, solitary aim" of this book? How does this apply to your life?

2. How does the author define "wisdom"? Are you walking in wisdom?

3. What is meant by the word "discipline"? Are you living a disciplined life?

4. How does the author describe Satan? In what specific ways does he work against you?

Day 1

"My master has withheld nothing from me except you, because you are his wife. How then could I do such a wicked thing and sin against God?" (Genesis 39:9).

Joseph, the most beloved of all Jacob's twelve sons, had already been through so much! As a result of a deep, dark bout of jealousy by his eleven brothers, Joseph was thrown into a dried-up well and left to die. Then he was mercifully retrieved from the well only to be bound and sold to a mercenary merchant caravan ambling through.

From there Joseph was transported far away from his cherished father and beloved homeland, only to endure the fear and humiliation of being passed off again to the highest bidder on the infamous Egyptian slave block. Yet, in his pitifully sad circumstance, was Joseph bitter toward God or Potiphar, his new earthly master? Amazingly, not in the least but maintained respect and righteousness towards them both.

At some point in Potiphar's service, Joseph's brawny, burnished body caught the eye of Potiphar's wife, and she propositioned him, "Come to bed with me!" (Genesis 39:7). Joseph immediately rebuffed her, saying, "My master has withheld nothing from me except you" (Genesis 39:9).

How reminiscent this is of our Lord's words to Adam: "You are free to eat from any tree in the garden; but you must not eat from the tree of the knowledge of good and evil, for when you eat of it you will surely die" (Genesis 2:16-17). So little does God actually restrict us from; and that which *is* off-limits is only restricted for our own good. "No good thing does he withhold from those whose walk is blameless" (Psalm 84:11).

Tantalizing allures of the Internet and impure images in print, film and television—each playing the part of Potiphar's wife—are calling out to us today, Brothers: "Come to bed with me!" And like courageous, righteous Joseph, we can and must resist: *God has withheld nothing from me except you!*

Tempting as it may have been, Joseph recognized that to indulge himself with Potiphar's wife was sinning first and foremost against God (see Psalm 51:4). He rhetorically asked, "How then could I do such a wicked thing and sin against God?"

Do you remember that breakthrough moment of illumination in the heart and mind of the Prodigal Son? It occurs when he's mulling over and over in his head, "Why any one of my father's hired men are better off than I am!" Next he determined that he should say to his father, "Father, I have sinned against heaven and against you" (Luke 15:18). He realized, as Joseph did, that all sin against others is actually first and foremost a sin against God.

There is another aspect to Joseph's resistance as well. Suffice that Joseph could have solely said to Potiphar's wife, "How … could I do such a wicked thing and sin against God?" Yet there is that far from inconsequential additional little word in there we must not overlook: "How *then* could I do such a wicked thing?" The word *then* is there in respect for Joseph's master, Potiphar—in regard to Potiphar's kindness toward Joseph and trust in him. Joseph said, in effect, "How then in response to my own fair treatment from Potiphar could I sin against *him*?"

How much greater than that is God's mercy and goodness toward each one of us! Our very breath He supplies, not to mention our salvation and incalculable other blessings. It immeasurably supersedes Potiphar's kind treatment toward Joseph. "Every good and perfect gift is from above" (James 1:17). When we are tempted sexually, we too would do well to ask ourselves: "How *then*, in light of God's great kindness, could I do such a wicked thing and sin against my God?"

---

1. How did Joseph resist Potiphar's wife when she invited him to come to bed with her?

2. What temptations in society today assume a role that is similar to the seductiveness of Potiphar's wife?

3. Against whom would Joseph have sinned had he gone to bed with Potiphar's wife?

4. What important question should you ask yourself when you are tempted sexually?

5. What are your sexual temptations?

DAY 2

"But I tell you that anyone who looks at a woman lustfully has already committed adultery with her in his heart" (Matthew 5:28).

The museum's curator knows where each and every item on exhibit is located—what it is exactly and in most cases what it is worth monetarily. In every greater respect, God is the human heart's Curator.

The Prophet Jeremiah cried out in sheer exasperation, "The heart is deceitful above all things and beyond cure. Who can understand it?" (Jeremiah 17:9). Our God can understand it, for He knows it fully. The Lord Jesus likewise "did not need man's testimony about man, for he *knew what was in a man*" (John 2:25).

In Matthew 5:28, Jesus explained to us that lust of the eyes for the male is indeed adultery—not by the letter of the Law but in spirit. God amply sees the sin, even though the woman sinned against may be thoroughly oblivious to its occurrence. Seeing our sin with none of its camouflage, God is fully apprised of the fact that we have managed to flaunt and trample on three of the Ten Commandments all at once.

Right off, we have broken the Second Commandment: "Thou shalt not make unto thee any graven image, or any likeness of any thing.... Thou shalt not bow down thyself to them, nor serve them: for I the LORD thy God am a jealous God" (Exodus 20:4-5, KJV). In the lusting over a woman, an unholy *image* has been formed in our minds. In the instances where Internet-based or other sources of pornography are viewed, that image is no longer in our imagination merely, but literal! In either case, an image, an idol, has been served and in effect been bowed down to.

Second and most obvious is that lust is a transgression of the Seventh Commandment:

"Thou shalt not commit adultery" (Exodus 20:14, KJV). Herein is the central point of Matthew 5:27-28, that the person who fantasizes impure actions with a woman has committed adultery with her, albeit "in his heart."

God is neither prude nor killjoy; it is simply that there is *unauthorized* and *unhealthy* sexuality God intends to exclude and from which He wants to protect us. God wants only what is best for us. Lust is a cheap substitute. God does not want us to miss out on His highest joys and highest purposes for our lives. And He demands that the precepts of His Holy Word be respected and uncompromised.

Thirdly, lust cavalierly discards the Tenth Commandment: "Thou shalt not covet thy neighbour's wife" (Exodus 20:17, KJV). Any one of us who has ever lusted or coveted has *desired another's wife*, even if she is not married presently. Were she never to marry, in fact, it is still wrong to covet that which is hers alone to offer up—her body and her sexual love. Knowing that we are prone to look for loopholes, God has left us none by summarizing in the Tenth Commandment: "Thou shalt not covet ... *any thing* that is thy neighbour's."

Even those with a secular worldview know what the term "playing with fire" means. All adulterous behavior (all the more so full-blown adultery affairs) were at one point instigated by mere lust, and therefore could have been prevented had lustful thinking not occurred and been acted on. Long before that undeniable bold red line was crossed into an adulterous affair, a hundred fainter, finer lines were ignored and traversed. The meaning here is that lustful rumination is not only a sin but is *playing with fire*. As the Proverb's author asked rhetorically on this very subject: "Can a man scoop fire into his lap without his clothes being burned?" (Proverbs 6:27).

The good news in all of this is that in addition to being our heart's Curator, the Lord truly is our divine Cardiologist. He alone is able to diagnose the true spiritual healthiness of our hearts and then is able to perform the spiritual surgical repair as required. He knows that regardless of what we might fake and feign in word or action, the *intentions of our heart* determine our soul's ultimate sickness or wellness. That is how He is able to say that he who looks upon a woman lustfully has committed adultery with her "in his heart."

God alone can peer into the deep recesses of our heart's intentions to diagnose and correct us. My Brothers, if you are lost in lust, coveting what belongs to a woman alone (and if she is married, what belongs to her husband), ask God to forgive you and to heal your heart.

1. Who is the "curator" of the human heart? Who is the "curator" of your heart?

2. In what ways is lusting after a woman a direct violation of the second, seventh and tenth commandments?

3. What should you do if you are lost in lust?

4. What opens the door to lust in your life?

DAY 3

"Then he said to them all: 'If anyone would come after me, he must deny himself and take up his cross daily and follow me'" (Luke 9:23).

Two remarkably different men appear in the dynamic theater of the gospels, yet either one of them *could have* become the thirteenth disciple. The first, the previously demon-possessed man of the ten-city region called the Decapolis, now with spirits dispossessed and in total serenity and solidarity of mind, pleaded with Jesus to become the thirteenth disciple. Jesus refused, instead instructing, "Go home to your family and tell them how much the Lord has done for you" (Mark 5:19).

The other candidate for the tiny band of apostles was a man who possessed every material amenity imaginable, known to us in biblical subheadings as "The Rich Young Ruler." In his case, Jesus did just the opposite and warmly extended the thrilling invitation, "Sell everything you have and give to the poor, and you will have treasure in heaven. Then *come, follow me*" (Luke 18:22).

Dejectedly, he slunk away. He did not fully comprehend the offer, for "what does it profit a man to gain the whole world and yet lose his very soul?) (Matthew 16:26, author's paraphrase). This much we do know: what he *did* comprehend was that Jesus was requiring that he *deny himself*. And that, tragically, he was unwilling to do.

In Luke 9:23 the universal siren to Christian discipleship is sounded: "If anyone would come after me, he must deny himself and take up his cross daily and follow me." Here we are shown that the undiluted, uncompromising pursuit of and passion for Jesus Christ as Lord and Savior involves these three requirements:

1) To deny oneself
2) To take up one's cross daily
3) To follow Him.

TO DENY ONESELF

This is the first mark of true discipleship. Are we willing to sacrifice and subjugate *any and all things* that impede and interfere with our obedience to Christ?

Each one of us, Brothers, has been deputized to follow the Master as He has told and taught us how. For our purposes here, are we unwilling to *deny ourselves* unrighteous and unauthorized sexual thoughts and experiences? If so, then we have abdicated our rights to the band and bonds of deputized disciples. Knowingly or unwittingly, we have surrendered our badge.

The Apostle Paul understood the cost of discipleship this way: "But whatever was to my profit I now consider loss for the sake of Christ. What is more, I consider everything a loss compared to the surpassing greatness of knowing Christ Jesus my Lord, for whose sake I have lost all things. I consider them rubbish, that I may gain Christ" (Philippians 3:7-8).

We would each one do well to surmise that unholy sexual circumstances and satisfactions are inconsequential to "the surpassing greatness of knowing Christ Jesus my Lord." There is *no comparison at all*; for these kinds of sins derail our discipleship and frankly are just not worth it!

TO TAKE UP ONE'S CROSS DAILY

It is fascinating to me that Jesus spoke these words *before* He went to the Cross! Who would have been surprised if Jesus had delivered this charter for true discipleship as He grilled the apostles' breakfast over the charcoal fire of John 21—*after* he had risen from the dead?

Surely it would have sunk in so much easier for them in that setting; that they too must walk in Christlike sacrificial love to the point of death—to carry their cross daily if necessary, as Jesus literally did to a cruel and ignoble death. After all, He had earlier taught, "Greater love has no one than this, that he lay down his life for his friends" (John 15:13); and now He had actually gone through with it!

And they had keenly observed the result of that sacrifice: "O death, where is thy sting? O grave, where is thy victory?" (1 Corinthians 15:55, KJV). Jesus had boldly triumphed over death, and His disciples could as easily have anticipated that death equally would neither conquer nor confine them. In light of that, this second requisite to true discipleship—to take up their cross daily—would make perfect sense.

But of course the campfire breakfast cooked up by the risen Lord is *not* when and where these words were spoken. Since this was *prior* to the Cross of Calvary, what were they to make of such language—to daily take up their cross?

They would have perceived it purely in view of the common occurrence of the condemned, each one carrying his cross to execution. To see it from that vantage point raises the bar still higher to the call of sacrificial, unwavering, slave-like devotion. If we are prepared and willing to carry our cross daily, one would think we would be willing to resist in the face of sexual temptations, even fierce ones.

TO FOLLOW HIM

The rich young ruler was no doubt reeling from the requirements of forsaking all; so much so that he barely even noticed that Jesus had said to come follow him. That little addendum meant *everything,* and he missed it! By following Jesus, he would be giving up nothing whatsoever. As Psalm 73:25 explains, earth has nothing to desire besides God.

The Apostle Peter was feeling both prideful and put out all at once when he complained, "We have left everything to follow you!" "I tell you the truth," Jesus replied, "no one who has left home or brothers or sisters or mother or father or children or fields for me and the gospel will fail to receive a hundred times as much in this present age (homes, brothers, sisters, mothers, children and fields—and with them, persecutions) and in the age to come, eternal life" (Mark 10:28-30).

To follow Jesus is all at once *protection, provision,* and *purpose.* Why, there is no better invitation in all of life! Shepherds lead sheep, and we are the sheep of His pasture (see Psalm 100:3). "Because the Lord is my shepherd, *I have everything I need*" (Psalm 23:1, The Living Bible).

When we are sexually unfulfilled, we need to turn to the Shepherd of our souls for strength and guidance. "It is God who arms me with strength and makes my way perfect" (Psalm 18:32). He "makes my way perfect." That doesn't mean free of problems; that means perfect as in the right and chosen pathways for me in order to fulfill his *perfect* plan for my life, in order that God would be most glorified.

In all venues of life we must remain a disciple of Jesus Christ, and no less in areas of our sexuality. When tempted with sexual impurity, we must *deny ourselves*, remembering our Lord has denied himself immeasurably *more* on our behalf.

When tempted with sexual impurity, we must *take up our cross daily*. And, unlike those doomed, despairing in their death march to a cruel ancient mode of execution, this is for us neither tragic nor a *one-time* event; but, as Christ says, it is something that must occur *daily*—a lifestyle of day-by-day obedience and subjection to Christ's will over our own.

Lastly and most of all, Brothers, when tempted with sexual impurity, we must *follow Him*; not our unrestrained impulses and appetites. He is truly the *One* who is happy to lead us and is most worthy of our following!

---

1. Which two men might have become the thirteenth disciple? Why?

2. What must you do in order to follow Jesus?

3. What is the cost of discipleship?

4. What are three of the blessings that come to those who decide to truly follow Jesus?

5. Have you decided to follow Him?

6. To whom should you turn when you feel sexually unfulfilled?

7. What must you do in order to avoid temptation of any kind?

Day 4

"For you have spent enough time in the past doing what pagans choose to do—living in debauchery, lust, drunkenness, orgies, carousing and detestable idolatry" (1 Peter 4:3).

"What benefit did you reap at that time from the things you are now ashamed of? Those things result in death!" (Romans 6:21).

Sometimes when I am tempted, I think of these verses, and they give me tremendous strength. They produce a tactical impediment to otherwise tumbling forward on a collision course toward the desired sin. When these passages come to mind, there is really only one alternative to their stopping me in my tracks; it is in effect to argue with the Bible's wisdom, making the defense that I have *not* "spent enough time" doing what the pagans choose to do! How ludicrous and foolhardy that sounds!

King David lamented, "For I know my transgressions, and my sin is always before me" (Psalm 51:3). Each one of us could make the same concession. We largely know *how* we have sinned and *how much* we have sinned. Because the Apostle Paul knew the answer, he posed his question, "What benefit did you reap at that time from the things you are now ashamed of?" He was confident that God's church in Rome whom he was addressing would know what the answer was. Indeed, the Holy Spirit knew that *future* believers (you and me reading this today, Brothers) would surely know the answer to how those things we are now ashamed of were of *no benefit* whatsoever!

Are we now to deceive ourselves into believing that somehow these things were good for us after all? Are we to delude ourselves into believing that *this time* delving into some kind of foray of sexual fantasies will be *different*—that truly we have *not spent enough time* doing such things?

Can we actually mean to say to the Holy Spirit, "Allow me to add but one more transgression to the list! *This time* it will accomplish the lasting satisfaction in my soul that has eluded me *every single time before*, solely producing shame, heartache, disappointment, and dismay." Such internal debate would be comical were it not so pitiful.

James, the Lord's earthly half-brother, had it so right when he said, "Then when lust hath conceived, it bringeth forth sin: and sin, when it is finished, *bringeth forth death*" (James 1:15, KJV). How similar James's insight is to this passage from the Psalms: "He who is pregnant with evil and conceives trouble *gives birth to disillusionment*" (Psalm 7:14).

Likewise, our selected passage today in Romans 6:21 concludes with these similarly chilling words: "Those things result in death!" That is what giving in to the Internet sirens of sin or any other male mental moral temptation has to offer us—disillusionment and death! I do not want death or disillusionment. I know that you don't either, Brothers.

Let us pray: Father, help us this day and each day to remember that we have spent far too much time in the past doing what the pagans do. And to what benefit? None whatsoever! Help us, Lord, to remember the end trail of sin that awaits us—disillusionment and death. Help us rather to choose holiness, contentment, and life! In Christ's name, Amen!

---

1. What benefits have you reaped from the things you are ashamed of?

2. How do you deal with any sense of shame in your life?

3. What happens to us when lust in conceived within our hearts?

4. How does lust lead to death?

Day 5

"No temptation has seized you except what is common to man. And God is faithful; he will not let you be tempted beyond what you can bear. But when you are tempted, he will also provide a way out so that you can stand up under it" (1 Corinthians10:13).

To take God at His word here is to believe that God wants us to be wholly victorious over temptation every time. We are not to be abject failures, ever falling into sin, controlled by sin, with little difference from the unredeemed man of our prior lives. God wants us to be changed, empowered—*successful*. And in this passage God is promising to assist us in such a way that we will always win. Did you hear me? I said *always win,* provided we want it bad enough. To look for, find, accept, and employ God's help at those moments means that when temptations come we will be able to "stand up under it" every single time!

The Apostle Paul instructed the slaves of ancient times who had become Christians, "If you can gain your freedom, do so" (1 Corinthians 7:21). In order for a Christian slave to take advantage of his freedom, however, he had to *recognize* it when it was offered. At each and every point of temptation, we are offered our freedom. The Scripture text we are examining here confidently reassures us that our God "will provide a way out." The question is: Do we believe this? Will we recognize the way out? Do we even *pause*, slow down at moments of our temptation, in order to pray—to see and find the way out God has provided?

There is a bodily pang that surpasses the physical pang for sexual satisfaction—the pang of hunger and thirst. Jesus felt it intensely; an unrelenting ache for hunger relief after his forty days of fasting. Many will say after several days of fasting that the pangs of hunger go away, but others will attest just as confidently that they never do go away entirely.

Have you ever fasted food (entirely, not eating a single morsel) for twenty, thirty, or forty days? I have not; but I have an extremely close and amazing friend who has done so on quite a few occasions. Each time he has attested that the hunger pangs for food never fully subsided.

That is what is corroborated here regarding Jesus's experience, when after forty days of fasting, Luke 4:2 describes that "he was hungry." This is why Satan did not appear with bags of gold or with a compliant, compromising woman in provocative apparel. Jesus's bodily need was plain and simple hunger, and that was exactly what Satan intended to exploit in challenging Jesus to turn stones into luscious, mouth-watering bread.

With uncanny consistency to our Corinthians passage today, God had earlier said in Deuteronomy 30:11, "What I am commanding you today *is not too difficult for you.*" Jesus knew this principle, and so He held strong.

Did you know that technically speaking Jesus did not have to? He could have said, "Devil, you really need a better timepiece. You're foolishly one single 24-hour day late! My forty-day fast has just been completed, and I have more than earned what you are suggesting."

But even though Jesus was eager to satisfy His body's justifiable demands, He was not willing to allow Satan to exalt himself over God and usurp God's will for His Son. So Jesus drew upon the strength within—the strength God has given each one of us as well—to remain faithful. He remembered and recited in faith to the devil, "Man does not live on bread alone but on every word that comes from the mouth of the LORD" (Deuteronomy 8:3; Luke 4:4).

When we are tempted, we are inclined to say, "This is too powerful for me!" But in truth, we are misinformed at those times. Jesus said in Matthew 22:29, "You are in error because you do not know the Scriptures or the power of God." To say, "This is too powerful for me" is to be misinformed in the Scriptures and misinformed regarding the power of God; for God has promised "He will not let you be tempted beyond what you can bear." God has promised to provide us with a way out! In order to escape, however, we must believe God is faithful, perceive the way out that He has provided, and then take it!

---

1. Is it possible for you to be totally victorious over sexual temptations? How?

2. How did Jesus counter the devil's temptations in the wilderness?

3. What must you believe in order to escape from temptation?

4. Are the temptations you face different from the temptations faced by other men?

Day 6

"Submit yourselves, then, to God. Resist the devil, and he will flee from you" (James 4:7).

We've all heard since our earliest infancy of individual Christian belief that "our struggle is not against flesh and blood, but against the rulers, against the authorities, against the powers of this dark world and against the spiritual forces of evil in the heavenly realms" (Ephesians 6:12). And it is absolutely true. The gauntlet has been thrown down. In terms of spiritual warfare, the gladiator games to the death have commenced.

Happily we know the final outcome; Satan loses, we win! (See Revelation 20:10 and 21:3-4.) Even so, until that final hour in which the devil and his dark angels are completely vanquished, we daily war in the spiritual realm with far from insignificant consequences in the *material* realm.

Sadly, most believers are not very skilled in the hand-to-hand combat the demonic players incite and engage us in. Perhaps we shall solve a very crucial missing piece to this common predicament here and now: I am convinced we are very often too quick to jump into the spiritual melee—too ambitious and urgent to "resist the devil"—going to Step 2 while never fully satisfying the prerequisite of Step 1.

The most important piece of instruction in James 4:7 is the part that is most often overlooked (usually not even quoted) when this passage, this spiritual principle, is discussed. That is, the *first part* of the verse is: "Submit yourselves, then, to God." So many times we have resisted the devil with great earnest, perhaps even great faith, and he seems not to even blink in the face of our resistance. At those times, we must ask God, "In what ways am I not submitting to you, Lord?"

The devil and his demons are powerless and unsurprisingly cowardly in any showdown with God (see James 2:19, Matthew 8:29). God will do His part, and the devil and his rodent servant spirits *will flee from us* as surely as this passage promises. The devil flees, however, only when he sees that it is a man *submissive to God* who is standing up to him. It is only at those times that the Archangel Michael's tactic of Jude 1:9 ("The Lord rebuke you!") may be employed by us mere humans, and at minimum we are able to pray to God with confidence, "Deliver us from the evil one" (Matthew 6:13).

Prepare yourself for this at least partial explanation to your *unsuccessful* spiritual warfare; if you are resisting God, the devil sees no reason to resist you. This bears repeating. *If you are resisting God the devil sees no reason to resist you!* And, if you are not resisting God, indeed, the devil is powerless to resist you!

James is not introducing a new idea in terms of how God wants us to cooperate with His deliverance in our lives. Speaking through the voice of His prophet Asaph in Psalm

81:13-14, God explained, "If my people would but listen to me, if Israel would follow my ways, how quickly would I subdue their enemies and turn my hand against their foes!"

In what ways are you resisting God today? Perhaps you readily know the answer to this. If not, God desires to reveal to you individually and precisely the answer. Do you even want to know the answer? God will show you when He knows you are *serious* about getting to the crux of your resistance and are ready and willing to fully yield to Him.

The Psalmist King David asked in Psalm 19:12a, "Who can discern his errors?" The question itself is replete with the answer: "No one fully." Not without God's help, that's for sure. David accordingly prayed next, "Forgive my *hidden* faults. Keep your servant also from willful sins" (Psalm 19:12b-13).

David recognized that there is so much we do not see, do not know, do not fully comprehend about the ways in which we offend the Lord. So he petitioned God, "Forgive my hidden faults"—those sins that were hidden to David himself but certainly not to God. And then to make sure all his bases were covered, David addressed the sins he was well aware he was committing: "Keep your servant also from willful sins."

If God will forgive us for our *hidden* sins and keep us from the *willful* or *deliberate* ones, we shall become more and more like Him—*holy*—and then someone fearful to the devil and quite prepared to resist him. David's prayer continued on that in *either* case, hidden or willful sins "may they not rule over me" (Psalm 19:13b). When these prayers are answered, we are in submission to God. When we are in submission to God, we may resist the devil; and he shall flee from us!

Let us pray: Father God, we have offended you so many times in so many ways. Many of them were hidden to us, but none of them to you. We are deficient in fully discerning our errors, although many of them we must concede are in fact willful. We earnestly desire to be holy and pure before you in the area of male mental moral purity. Please forgive our hidden faults; above all keep us from the willful ones, and let neither hidden nor willful sins rule over us. Please allow the devil to see our lives in such submission to you that the tempter must flee from us as we resist him! In Christ's name, Amen.

---

1. What two steps must you take before the devil will flee from you?

2. Against what kinds of forces must you wage spiritual warfare?

3. What does full submission to God entail?

4. Are you submitted to God in all areas of your life?

5. In what ways are you resisting God today?

6. From what types of sins did David seek to be forgiven?

Day 7

"For the grace of God that brings salvation has appeared to all men. It teaches us to say 'No' to ungodliness and worldly passions, and to live self-controlled, upright and godly lives in this present age" (Titus 2:11-12).

Nancy Reagan, the most elegant of first ladies, is credited during her husband's presidency with creating the slogan and positive anti-drug campaign aimed at kids, "Just Say No." Its goal was to provide kids the impetus and a tool in order to reject dangerous, illegal, recreational drug use. God, of course, delivered his own *very first* "Just Say No" campaign to *His* kids, Adam and Eve in the Garden of Eden.

Nancy Reagan's anti-drug-use campaign was modestly effective and no doubt has continued to this day to do some tangible good. Yet here in Titus is something so much more potent than any slogan and government advertising blitz. We are talking about the grace of God. It is that *grace* that "teaches us to say 'No' to ungodliness and worldly passions" (verse 11).

It is sad and even shocking to some degree that any one of us Christian men would ever need support in this way in the areas of lust or pornography. One would think that anything as primal, unseemly, and ungodly would hold no appeal to the *regenerated* man. The truth is, however, that if all worldly passions were extinguished entirely at the point of salvation, we would be immortal, and these admonitions in Scripture would have no point to them.

We are being taught how to say "'No' to ungodliness and worldly passions" because God's Word is conceding here that these temptations can stubbornly hang on. Elsewhere the Apostle Paul admonished God's Church, "Do not let sin reign in your mortal body so that you obey its evil desires" (Romans 6:12). Paul would not have had to give this dictum if the evil desires had completely ceased to exist. Unfortunately, this side of Heaven they can be very resilient.

Still, take heart, my Brothers, that God will not ask anything of us that He has not prepared and equipped us to accomplish successfully in our lives. When His Word says, "Do not let sin reign in your mortal body so that you obey its evil desires," it means *we do not have to!* We do not have to allow sin to reign in us! We don't have to obey sin's evil desires! We can "*Just Say Noooooo!*"

God transcends time. He knows the end from the beginning and everything in between. He has not been caught off-guard by the onslaught of immorality on our television and in our movie theatres and that today is so readily accessible on our computers. Sometimes we act as if we are thinking, "If only God had known how bad it was going to get!" He knew, He knows, and He has a solution for it. The solution is *himself.*

He is here for us, and He will guide and empower us to overcome—*today!*

How do we know this still works? Look at that little phrase at the end of our passage: "in this present age." God put that in there because He knew that until Christ returns, Christians will read this and in turn apply this to our *own specific times,* to our *own specific problems*, and to our *own specific needs* in our *own present age.*

God is promising that His grace, the grace that "brings salvation" and which has "appeared to all men," will teach us how to do the things we need to do most in achieving male mental moral purity—as Paul says to Titus in our text today, that we would "live self-controlled, upright and godly lives *in this present age*."

---

1. What does God's grace teach us to do?

2. To what types of things must you learn to say no?

3. How are we supposed to be living in this present age?

4. Is your daily life God-centered?

Day 8

"Be still, and know that I am God; I will be exalted among the nations, I will be exalted in the earth" (Psalm 46:10).

Sometimes it seems like the hardest thing on earth to do is just to be still—to be absolutely inactive, quiet, patient, compliant, to take no action whatsoever, to do nothing, to be *still.* In truth, this biblical admonition is not about doing nothing exactly, but doing *nothing more* than to be simply still before the Lord. This means to be exclusively attentive to God and His voice rather than to the noisy clatter all about us and all the noisier inner tantrums of the flesh.

Even though it goes against our nature to be still, Christians must have romanticized the notion to the point that we actually think we are good at it, because we quote this verse a lot. Virtually never, however, are the verses before it and immediately subsequent to it quoted at the same time. That is unfortunate, for it is in its broader context within the Psalm that we fully absorb its aid and application, its serene efficacy regarding our *daily battles*—most pertinent to us here in the pursuit of personal purity. The preceding and subsequent verses read:

Psalm 46:9: "He makes wars cease to the ends of the earth; he breaks the bow and shatters the spear, he burns the shields with fire."

And then Psalm 46:11: "The LORD Almighty is with us; the God of Jacob is our fortress."

Have you ever felt your struggle for purity is no minor struggle but an all-out *war* in your mind and soul? Then remember: "He makes wars *cease* to the ends of the earth.... Be still, and know that I am God."

Have you ever felt like the bows and spears and shields of Satan and the world are all aimed at you personally with the one goal being your moral failure, in fact your entire spiritual destruction? Then remember: "He *breaks* the bow and *shatters* the spear, he *burns* the shields with fire.... Be still, and know that I am God."

Have you ever felt totally alone in your struggle? Then remember: "The LORD Almighty *is with us*." "Be still, and know that I am God.

Have you ever wished there were some place to escape, somewhere you could go and hide, to feel safe and secure and wholly protected? A place where the attacks could not even penetrate? A place that could only be described as a *fortress*? Then remember: "The God of Jacob is our fortress." "Be still, and know that I am God."

In the area of male mental moral purity, to be still and know that *God is God* becomes a very valuable resource—a tried and true, reliable biblical strategy for deliverance. There have been many times when I have been under attack and have been merely still before the Lord. The attack has receded; and then, if I have remained still just a little bit longer, it has retreated and then vanished from whence it came. Let God be exalted among the nations! Let God be exalted in the earth! "Be still, and know that I am God."

---

1. What must you do in order to be still before the Lord?

2. In what ways do the verses immediately preceding and following Psalm 46:10 relate to its main theme?

3. God says, "I will be exalted among the nations, I will be exalted in the earth." How does this statement relate to our battle against sexual temptation?

4. Do you take time each day to be still before the Lord?

Day 9

"The widow who lives for pleasure is dead even while she lives" (1 Timothy 5:6).

This thirty-one day devotional book is aimed at *men*, not widows, so why should we explore a verse such as this? Because at its core is a principle from which we men can learn an awful lot. Much of the fifth chapter of 1 Timothy is devoted to rules for the care and eligibility of "widows," but within this verse is a principle that applies to any person at all. That principle is this: *The person who lives for pleasure is already dead.*

This may be hyperbole, exaggerated language the Apostle Paul has employed in order to make his strongest point possible. Yet, it is a very sobering thought. When we live for pleasure—*when we make choices to accommodate the desire for temporal and temporary sensual satisfaction over obeying God*—we may as well be dead!

We've all heard unbelievers describe Christians as "nothing more than a bunch of hypocrites." That is largely an unfair, overreaching generalization; and certainly it is an accusation levied not to challenge us to exhibit lives that more accurately exemplify the Lord, but is more likely spewed to deflect the spotlight off their own darkened souls and conscience-burdened actions.

Still, sadly, we must concede there are many times when the charge is well-deserved. In those instances, there is no one more concerned and more vigilant to exfoliate the forgery, more interested in evoking change in the person, than *the Lord.* Among other things, Jesus boldly exposed such religious fakes as "whitewashed tombs," saying to their very faces, "You hypocrites!" (Matthew 23:27).

Today, as then, these are people who are extremely *outwardly* religious—persons who have gotten "Churchianity" down pat. They know precisely when to say "Praise the Lord!" and to be deemed most spiritual. They are well-skilled in crinkling their brow and looking most solemn when they say, "I'll pray for you."

They even know which church events to show up for, versus the ones when their absence will likely go unnoticed or at minimum least likely to be critiqued unfavorably. All the while, they appear "beautiful on the outside but on the inside are full of dead men's bones and everything unclean" (Matthew 23:27). And this is all because they are most interested in securing "praise from men more than praise from God" (John 12:43).

God forbid, Brothers, that *any one of us* should look just grand on the outside—saying and doing all the right things at church and in front of our Christian friends—while on the inside we are *dead*, or may as well be, because in truth we are living for pleasure! This is exactly what happens—what we slowly but steadily become when we give in to the titillating lies and lures of sexual temptation Satan strategically places before us on a nearly daily basis.

Christ has proclaimed, "I am the vine; you are the branches. If a man remains in me and I in him, he will bear much fruit; apart from me you can do nothing. If anyone does not remain in me, he is like a branch that is thrown away and withers; such branches are picked up, thrown into the fire and burned" (John 15:5-6).

When we give in to Internet porn, sex and nudity in movies, or otherwise induced impure thoughts, we are both without fruit and uprooted from the Lord (what Jude 1:12 calls "*twice dead*"). We have voluntarily cut ourselves off from the true Vine, Jesus Christ. *Incapable* now of bearing fruit and being cut off from God (the source of our life-sustaining nourishment), we spiritually wither and die. May we never live for pleasure, my Brothers, but instead always live for the Lord!

---

1. What is the thematic principle of this particular devotion? How does it apply to your life?

2. What happens when one gives in to Internet porn and/or sex and nudity in movies and magazines?

3. What must you do in order to be a fruitful Christian? Are you a fruit-bearing Christian?

4. Do others see Jesus in your life?

Day 10

"If your right eye causes you to sin, gouge it out and throw it away. It is better for you to lose one part of your body than for your whole body to be thrown into hell" (Matthew 5:29).

Jesus presented this rather unsettling mental picture immediately after His startling pronouncement that he who "looks at a woman lustfully has already committed adultery with her in his heart" (Matthew 5:28). Jesus was trying His best to make sure the seriousness of this sin is neither overlooked nor in the least minimized. He additionally gave a prescription for its avoidance.

Is it the eye that is offending and sinning when lust is occurring? If so, then Jesus was saying, "Get rid of that organ of the body!" But then, is it the eye that is sinning?

First off, no sane person would dare gouge out one or both of his eyes. No! In fact, ironically, by using such a gory, implausible example Jesus was highlighting the fact that it is *not* the eye that is sinning. It is you! It is me! It is *the heart!* Jesus had only seconds before made it perfectly clear that the person who has sinned in this way is committing adultery "*in his heart*." Those were Jesus' exact words.

Now that we've placed the discussion in its vital context, how must we respond? We must *redirect the heart,* and to do that we must not trifle with this issue. Lust is too ferocious, too unwieldy, and (at first) untamable to be taken lightly. We have to approach this thing as Jesus implored us to—as if our very eternal destiny depended on it!

Jesus was in effect saying, "Let's be logical about this. As horrific and excruciating it would be to gouge one's eyes out—awful and inexplicable to become *deliberately* blinded—it would be *far worse* to go merrily to hell with both eyes in perfect working order!"

And of course he was right. Given the choice between that extreme pain and loss here and now but granted the reward of eternal life or *foregoing* that irrevocable impairment but receiving eternal damnation and the terrors of hell, any thinking male would instantly choose the hot iron rod that Sampson faced (Judges 16:21). Blessed be the Lord, we are not *literally* faced with that quandary!

That said, Brothers, are we willing to employ (as Jesus was advising) *extreme measures* in order to maintain righteous and pure thoughts toward women? Are we willing to spend a little bit more money in order to have an adequate Internet filter on our computers? Are we willing to have a Christian brother set it up without our knowing its password to prevent its discretionary *disabling*? Are we willing to expose our level of temptations and failures to our pastors or some other stronger Christian brother for prayer support, strategy, and accountability? You get the idea.

Gouging out our eyes, so to speak, means taking actions that are *severe*—probably representing a legitimate loss of money, pride, and such—in order to honor God and put a red-alert priority on personal vigilance in this area. To act otherwise is to respond pretty unconcerned and nonchalant toward something God is not at all flippant about. If He were, He would not have given us the dramatic and gruesome example Jesus gave us in Matthew 5:29. And that is not a pretty picture.

---

1. What commandment of Jesus immediately precedes Matthew 5:29?

2. Have you ever been ensnared by Internet pornography?

3. Are you willing to spend the necessary money to install an adequate Internet pornography filter on your computer?

4. Are you willing to have a Christian brother install an adequate Internet pornography filter on your computer?

Day 11

"I will set before my eyes no vile thing" (Psalm 101:3).

Perhaps God in his own divine foresight allowed the inventors of TV to call it the "television *set*" with this scriptural principle in mind. Think about it: "I will *set* before my eyes."

Regardless, it is an interesting coincidence of sorts.

Certainly television has been a great purveyor of "vile" things for many years, from its prolific vulgar language to scenes of nudity and sexual situations, and from its brazen pro-gay agenda to innumerable assorted anti-God and immoral plot lines. And I'm just thinking about the standard fare of the major networks, to say nothing of the far less restricted immorality smorgasbord on pay-per-view cable movies.

The trouble is not TV, however. The trouble is not movies, Hollywood big business, or the Internet. The trouble is *us*! The trouble is the inclinations of our hearts, the inclination of hearts when uninclined and unresponsive toward God.

All of the above industries and mediums only sell what we buy, what *we want.* It is that basic. They would clean up their act in a New York minute if our entertainment appetites were transformed to the point that we no longer desired their garbage and no longer watched it when it is offered. Like the Prodigal Son in Luke 15:16, the typical entertainment consumer is, spiritually speaking, so far from home that he longs to fill his belly with what the pigs are eating!

The truth is that, if we didn't watch, the advertisers underwriting these mediums would be forced to spend their dollars elsewhere in support of cleaner programming because their current target audiences who are buying their products would not be there any more. For now, sadly, they have no such inclination or incentive, for "The wicked *freely strut about* when what is vile is *honored among men*" (Psalm 12:8).

In Psalm 101, God put the burden of making our homes a smut-free zone squarely on our *own* shoulders. In declaring, "*I will* set before my eyes no vile thing" (verse 3), the Psalmist (King David) was taking personal responsibility. And he went even further to reinforce this in the verses just prior and subsequent to it. Verse 2 reads, "*I will* be careful to lead a blameless life—when will you come to me? *I will* walk in my house with blameless heart." And then verse 4 continues, "Men of perverse heart shall be far from me; *I will* have nothing to do with evil."

It takes constant effort to be pure before the Lord. This whole thirty-one day devotional is about taking on an ardent work ethic about this. It should be very encouraging to us that King David modeled this for us.

David said, "I will *be careful* to lead a blameless life." It doesn't happen automatically, Brothers. He was committing his own willpower and determination to produce the desired outcome in his life, and yet simultaneously (and in such precious fashion) was acknowledging his utter *dependence upon God* as he called out for God's help, "When will you come to me?" Without God, no success would be possible. On that basis David dedicated himself to this righteous course: "I will walk *in my house* with blameless heart."

Would it be fair to say that people writing, producing, and performing in perverse ways for the purpose of our supposed entertainment, could be characterized as "men of perverse heart?" If so, then we need to rethink whether we should be so happily near to them, *embracing* their products—*paying* for their products. Or, like David, should we prefer to have them and their filthy wares far away from us? David said, "Men of perverse heart shall be far from me."

In the fourth instance in this Psalm, King David took *personal responsibility* for his righteous environment and righteous choices, pledging, "I will have nothing to do with evil." Will we this day pledge the same?

Let us pray: Father God, please forgive us, for we have not been blameless in terms of vile things we have knowingly set before our eyes or at the very least not averted our eyes away from. Give us the determination of King David to walk blameless in our own homes. Keep purveyors of perversity far from us and help us to have nothing to do with evil. Last of all—*first* of all really—Lord, we need *more of you*. We echo David's entreaty: *When will you come to us*? In Christ's name, Amen.

---

1. In what way is the typical entertainment consumer of today like the Prodigal Son in the New Testament?

2. What are the four things that David, the Psalmist, says he will do (in Psalm 101:3-4)? Is this an example that you should be following?

3. Are you willing to pledge, as David did, “I will have nothing to do with evil”?

4. Are there specific impure media influences in your life that you need to avoid?

Day 12

"Watch and pray so that you will not fall into temptation" (Matthew 26:41).

If this devotional were limited to only three or four Scriptures for reflection instead of thirty-one passages, we would certainly have to include this one. Leave it to our Lord Jesus to so succinctly distill the remedy for temptation down to these two simple and most salient things:

1) Watch, *so that you will not fall into temptation*; and

2) Pray, *so that you will not fall into temptation.*

Watch for what? For the obvious temptations and for the *not so obvious*. Remember that Satan, personified in the form of a serpent, was the most "crafty" of all God's creatures (Genesis 3:1). The King James Bible casts a slightly different but perhaps more enlightening nuance to the serpent's predominant characteristic in the events of the Garden. It calls him the most "subtle." The Apostle Paul says the devil is apt to appear as "an angel of light" in an attempt to sway us through the most *un*obvious means (2 Corinthians 11:14).

Temptation is continually coming at us. And then after it has come—*Watch,* for it is coming back again! Jesus was not tempted by Satan's minions (some undersecretary of the demon world) but was tempted by Satan *himself*—standing there in living color. And after Jesus gave Satan a thorough dressing down, utterly reducing and rebuffing him, the Bible says the devil "left him *until an opportune time*" (Luke 4:13).

Satan was down but not out. He was leaving with his ego bruised, head drooped, and pointy tail between his legs, but the Word confirms for us the devil would, nonetheless, surely strike again. God directly promised the devil to his face that ultimately Jesus Christ (the "seed" of Eve) would "crush [his] head" (Genesis 3:15), but this was not that hour, and so Satan would regroup to look and to linger for his next best opportunity.

The devil and his demons are that way with us as well. Matthew and Paul did not call Satan "the tempter" (Matthew 4:3, 1 Thessalonians 3:5) without good reason—he tempts! And when he is successfully repudiated by our faith and the Word of God, he has not (this side of Heaven) ever resigned himself to leaving us alone entirely but has only been removed for the time being—until his next "opportune time."

Jesus implores us, therefore, to stand guard! Don't fall asleep at your watch post! If you do, the results may be disastrous. "Your enemy the devil prowls around like a roaring lion looking for someone to devour" (1 Peter 5:8). He wants to devour our faith. Unfortunately, one of the quickest, fastest-acting ways he can cut us down to size is with inciting *lust*—particularly aided by pornographic, or merely sensuous, imagery.

The Apostle Paul said, "We are not unaware of his schemes" (2 Corinthians 2:11). Can we say the same thing? I fear not, Brothers. It is as if we have been lured into the lion's den thinking there is a cuddly, cozy kitten in there instead of a hungry, hostile man-eater.

Watch! Do not be naïve nor reckless about the things that draw you into temptation. Are you strong enough to go to the beach on a hot summer day? Only you and God know the answer to that. Are you wise and strong enough to flip to another station when a lingerie commercial comes on? Can you hit the skip button the moment the sex scene is starting its set up (not actually begun) in the movie on your DVD player? Let's be honest, Men; in most cases, the films give us sufficient *advance* notice.

Are you disciplined enough to gaze down at the floor or to go get some popcorn during scenes of sex or nudity at the theater? The examples could go on and on, but you get the point.

"Pray … that you will not fall into temptation" is the other half of Jesus' instruction here and very reminiscent of Jesus's sample prayer: "And lead us not into temptation" (Matthew 6:13; Luke 11:4) from what is commonly called The Lord's Prayer.

The Lord does not tempt us (James 1:13) but since we view Him, indeed *implore* Him, to be the overarching guiding force and protector over our lives—the *one who leads us*—it is only prudent Jesus would beckon us into prayers that we be not led into temptation and not fall into temptation. The Lord desires to navigate us *away* from persons, places, powers, and circumstances that might exploit areas of weakness in us. How sorely we need this, for who could dispute what

Jesus concisely defined as our universal vulnerability: "The spirit is willing, but the body is weak (Matthew 26:41)"?

When Jesus says, "Pray so that you will not fall into temptation," He is *not* merely saying, "Pray these precise words and you will be safe." He is teaching us this in the broader context of the other things God has to say to us about an effectual prayer life. He is saying pray for this (that you will not fall) with *faith* (Mark 11:24, James 1:6); pray for this as much as possible at the *earliest* start in your day (Mark 1:35); pray for this when you can steal away from the urgent demands of each day's responsibilities—for *long periods* (Luke 6:12); and pray for this with *regularity* (Acts 3:1).

Pray for this with *persistence* (Luke 11:5-10); pray for this *fervently* (James 5:17, KJV). Pray *not* with selfish motives but with the prime motive of glorifying God and with *humility* (James 4:3 and 6). Pray with an attitude of *thanksgiving* (Philippians 4:6). And, at least some of the time pray with one, two, or more *prayer partners* (Matthew 18:19; Acts 12:12).

If you are on a treadmill going nowhere in terms of moral purity thinking and behavioral improvement, consider these guidelines for effective alertness to temptation and regarding your prayer life. Then ask yourself, "Am I watching and praying?"

---

1. Jesus said, "Watch and pray so that you will not fall into temptation" (Matthew 26:41). Specifically, what should you be watching for?

2. Who is the most "crafty" of all God's creatures?

3. What are some of the biblical metaphors and similes that relate to Satan?

4. What elements of prayer should you incorporate into your prayer life in order to obey Jesus's commandment that is found in Matthew 26:41?

5. Are you watching and praying each day?

Day 13

"Elijah went before the people and said, 'How long will you waver between two opinions? If the LORD is God, follow him; but if Baal is God, follow him.' But the people said nothing" (1 Kings 18:21).

Baal was the most prominent of all Old Testament idols, most likely for this simple reason that he was the "god of rain." In the Middle-Eastern world (much of it very arid), and at that time in history (pre-modern irrigation ingenuity) dependence on rain was something akin to dependence on air—pretty much non-negotiable to survival. Thus, in a society uninformed about or uninterested in worshiping the *true* Lord (Yahweh), it was not in the least surprising that they devised a god who was responsible for rain—who dispensed rain upon his own whims and appeasement.

Unremarkable as that may be, Elijah is not amused nor slightly tolerant of their vain, pointless, *apostate* religion. If rain is what is needed, then only the true Lord, Maker of Heaven and earth, is to be consulted and petitioned! That is why Elijah challenged his kindred Israelites (ones who *should have known better*), "How long will you waver between two opinions?"

Elijah simplified things for them saying, "If the Lord is God, follow him; but if Baal is God, follow him." The rest of the story is really worth reading and re-reading for Elijah went further than his arresting challenge to them and demonstrated in very courageous, miraculous, and *undeniable* fashion just which One true God was real and worthy of their undivided worship and devotion.

When we are drawn into the world of lust or porn, even its mildest forms, we need to say to ourselves as Christian men, "How long will you waver between two opinions? If Eros—the Greek god of *erotic* pleasures—is god, *follow him*; but if the Lord is God, follow him!"

Satan, and our own resilient traces of fallen man within, would seduce us at moments of temptation into believing that sexual pleasure is as vital as air or water. It's not! So let's use our heads for a moment, Brothers; take Elijah's advice and get off the fence. Which one is God? Stop wavering between two opinions and choose.

Jesus said similarly in Matthew 6:24, "No one can serve two masters. Either he will hate the one and love the other, or he will be devoted to the one and despise the other." James 1:8 teaches us as well that the double-minded man is unstable in everything he does.

One of the last things Jesus ever said in the Bible was, "I know your deeds, that you are neither cold nor hot. I wish you were one or the other!" (Revelation 3:15). Like Elijah before him, Jesus dared us to make up our minds! And if we will not, he continued, "So because you are lukewarm—

neither hot nor cold—I am about to spit you out of my mouth" (Revelation 3:16).

Like those tepid believers Jesus rebuked in Revelation, our passage of study today records the *astounding* silence: "But *the people said nothing*." Elijah desperately wanted to see them to get off the fence, to choose between their "two opinions." They were neither hot nor cold, however, and therefore "said nothing."

Let us pray: Lord Jesus, we choose you and you alone. We love you, and we want no part of the false god Eros, worldly erotica, and all things Satan and our own recalcitrant, frail, human tendencies would find to deceive us into believing that impurity is beneficial at *any* level. Please forgive us for all the times we have been of two opinions in this matter. Shore us up to be *red hot* for you, steadfast in our heart's single-mindedness to follow you and you alone. In your name we pray, Amen.

---

1. Which idol in the Old Testament was the most prominent of all?

2. Do you have any idols in your life?

3. Are you wavering between two opinions? If so, what should you do about it?

4. What is the inevitable result of being double-minded?

5. Are you hot, cold, or lukewarm in your relationship with the Lord?

Day 14

"When I saw that they were not acting in line with the truth of the gospel, I said to Peter in front of them all, 'You are a Jew, yet you live like a Gentile and not like a Jew. How is it, then, that you force Gentiles to follow Jewish customs?" (Galatians 2:14).

Naturally, each of us genuinely wants our life to be a vibrant, living testimony to the truth and vitality of the gospel. We are Christian men, after all, and our Lord has commanded, "Go into all the world and preach the good news to all creation" (Mark 16:15). We want to see others come to faith in Christ as we did. That said, when any single aspect of our lives invalidates or even modestly undermines the truth and power of that gospel, we severely diminish the effectiveness of our witness.

Paul cut straight to the heart when he saw that Peter was "not acting in line with the truth of the gospel." No matter how well we disguise it, no matter how hard we pretend the sin issue isn't present in our lives, we know (and God surely knows) when we are not acting in line with the truth of the gospel. Our witness is inauthentic at those times and consequently of little to no spiritual fruit-bearing.

In effect, Paul was saying to Peter, "You can't have it both ways! You can't live as if you're not a Jew, all the while imploring others to embrace the Jewish religion." The same goes for us Christians. We can't be passionately advocating others to come to saving faith in Christ—to turn from sin and turn from living for self toward living for God—when it's actually *not working for us*. When there's that kind of discrepancy in our lives, we reduce our once vibrant, authentic testimony to sullen silence. Or, the other alternative is we speak out as fervently as ever, simultaneously *cringing* inside from the blubbering hypocrisy ringing out in our own heads.

Christ wants us to be his witnesses. Acts 1:8 shares the immense confidence-building news that we shall "receive power" for the task. The Lord Jesus has left us the Holy Spirit in order to accomplish this (see John 20:22). Jesus himself is no longer on earth in the flesh; yet mysteriously He is! He is here in us, in His Church, by His Spirit living within us: "Christ *in you*, the hope of glory" (Colossians 1:27; see Matthew 28:20b). And because of this fantastic fact, there is no need for timidity. "For God did not give us a *spirit of timidity*, but a spirit of power; of love and of self-discipline" (2 Timothy 1:7). The very next verse tells us for what purpose: "So (in light of this fact that you possess *God's own Spirit* of power, love, and self-discipline within you) do not be ashamed *to testify* about our Lord" (verse 8).

If we are not right with the Lord, if we are living some kind of phony double life, we will be rightly ashamed to testify to the Lord in our lives—the very thing 2 Timothy 1:8

is urging us to do. Thankfully, this same Spirit that accounts for our *boldness* is also present within us to empower us (according to 2 Timothy1:7) with *self-discipline* in order to shore up, accomplish, and preserve our *righteous* witness.

Jesus said, "You are the salt of the earth. But if the salt loses its saltiness, how can it be made salty again? It is no longer good for anything, except to be thrown out and trampled on by men" (Matthew 5:13). We are to season the world with the hope and truth of the gospel and, like salt, create a *thirst* in our hearers for the only One who is able to quench the vacant, parched soul and spirit.

When we participate in areas of impurity, we are the ones who are spiritually dry. And it doesn't take a lot of impurity to be impure. We don't have to be addicted to porn. Even our chronic mild accommodations to the lusts of the flesh can derail God's will and work in our lives. "A little yeast works through the whole batch of dough" (Galatians 5:9; see Mark 4:19).

It is at those times that we have lost our saltiness, and how may we regain it? Only by repentance, by God's grace and God's mercy. Otherwise our testimonies are "thrown out" (Matthew 5:13). In a court of law it would be viewed as *inadmissible*—not enough true factual evidence to convict—and have set ourselves up to having our witness (like savorless salt) "trampled on."

Instead of a silenced witness (or worse yet, a *hypocritical* witness), Brothers, we need our purity restored, our hearts renovated, our faith renewed, and a righteously—*factually correct*—witness "in line with the truth of the gospel." For this we pray, heavenly Father. In Christ's name, Amen.

---

1. Are you obeying the Great Commission of Jesus?

2. What has God provided in order to enable you to be a powerful witness for Christ?

3. What is your hope of glory?

4. Why did God give you a spirit of power, love, and self-discipline?

5. Are you the "salt of the Earth"? What does this mean to you?

6. If you lose your "saltiness," how can you regain it?

7. What are the properties of salt? How does this apply to your life?

Day 15

"His divine power has given us everything we need for life and godliness through our knowledge of him who called us by his own glory and goodness" (2 Peter 1:3).

It is so easy to feel incomplete, dissatisfied about our finances, our kids, our career, our sex life, our marriage or singlehood, our church, our health, our looks, our in-laws, our sense of accomplishment (especially after about forty-five or fifty), our golf score, our make and model of car … blah blah blah blah blah. Satan's mischief and our own mixed potion of self-pride and self-pity can make us innately pretty discontented folk. When that is our predominant individual disposition in life, we can be very miserable inside and at minimum vulnerable to the need for some added excitement—receptive to a little *unholy* excitement for our lives.

This Scripture passage is the antidote for this. The Lord's divine power "has given us *everything we need* for life and godliness." How reminiscent it is to the beloved Psalm 23 and its opening stanza: "The LORD is my shepherd, I shall not be in want." How can we be lacking and unfulfilled when

He has provided everything we need *for life?* That pretty much covers everything!

I know it takes faith to always absorb this truth, and I am far from fully mature in this, Brothers, but then as the Apostles once said to our Lord Christ, "Increase our faith!" (Luke 17:5). Or as the father of the demonized child exclaimed to our Lord, "I do believe; help me overcome my unbelief!" (Mark 9:24).

Day by day we must work on believing and retaining this truth that will immeasurably help us in our steadfastness and pursuit of personal purity. If God's divine power has given us everything we need for life, then we should be content, full, satisfied—which means no longer restless and intent on adding *excitement* to our mundane lives.

According to this passage, "his divine power" is what *enables us* to lead the kinds of lives He wants for us—the lives we want for ourselves—in terms of personal godliness and holiness. His divine power (not a power from within our human spirits or emanating from any pop psychology, latest books, fad teachers, or any other external source, but from God alone) has given us "everything we need for life *and godliness*."

When a demon whispers in the night, "You can't do it," or we murmur to our very own souls, "I can't do it," we are misinformed. *We can do it!* By "his divine power" and by something else this passage teaches: We can do this "through *our knowledge of him* who called us by his own glory and goodness."

How is your *knowledge of Him* who's called you? Perhaps spiritually speaking you are still an infant when you should be mature by now. God forbid that the scathing indictment of Hebrews 5:12 fits any one of us when it says: "Though by this time you ought to be teachers, you need someone to teach you the elementary truths of God's word all over again. You need milk, not solid food!"

The writer of Hebrews 5:12-14 was visibly agitated because he saw a need for retraining in *righteousness* and in the ability to "distinguish good from evil" (the very thing we are striving for in this thirty-one day devotional). It was something he believed they should have long before then become mature in, something he considered "*elementary* truths."

Perhaps you haven't read God's Word (the four Gospels in particular) lately or nearly that much at all in your Christian life and have only a cursory, introductory knowledge of *Him who's called you*. Get more! Dive into the Gospels anew! You will be appropriating His divine power for greater godliness in your life as you *gain more knowledge of Jesus*. It's promised here! Alas, with this knowledge, Brothers, we may live lives that demonstrate having all that we need for life and godliness.

---

1. What has God's divine power given to you?

2. How extensive is your knowledge of Him who has called you? Do you spend time with Him each day?

3. Do you study the Word of God daily? Why do you need to do so?

DAY 16

"Blessed are the pure in heart, for they will see God" (Matthew 5:8).

To see God is the ultimate goal for all of us. To be with Him in Heaven for eternity when the curse of Eden is lifted, where we will serve Him, and where we will see God—literally, behold His face. "No longer will there be any curse. The throne of God and of the Lamb will be in the city, and his servants will serve him. They will see his face, and his name will be on their foreheads" (Revelation 22:3-4).

Jesus's Sermon on the Mount with its Beatitudes was most revolutionary. Teaching that it is blessed of all things to be *persecuted*, that merely to hate someone is to commit *murder*, to lust is to commit *adultery*, that the "meek" (versus the domineering) shall inherit the earth, that a writ of divorce for any and all reasons is no longer permissible; that it's required to reconcile with the *human* you've offended before presenting your gifts in worship and reconciliation to the divine, to no longer make oaths (an ancient and revered tradition) but merely make your simple declaration of "yes" or "no" fully suffice; to love your *enemies*, to consider that blessed are those who *mourn* versus the joyous, and so on and so on were all totally counterintuitive to Jesus's listeners that day. They still are to us.

But in the midst of all those challenging, provocative words (perplexing and *compelling* all at once) there is this little oasis of truth that would have found no objectioners: "Blessed are the pure in heart, for they will see God." What Jesus was saying here was something they genuinely *longed to hear* but only *dared* to believe could come true! Jesus was saying in effect, "Blessed are the pure in heart, for they shall see God and *not be killed* for seeing God!"

The ancients were *afraid* to see God, for they knew God was holy and that they were not! Manoah, the mighty Samson's father, told his wife, "We are doomed to die! . . . We have seen God!" (Judges 13:22).

Now, of course, Moses saw the Lord in Exodus 34 without dying; and there were other exceptions, particularly when the Lord was manifested as the "angel of the Lord" (see Hagar's encounter in Genesis 16, Balaam's in Numbers 22, and Elijah's in 2 Kings 1); but with or without concrete evidence to confirm these exceptions, the prevailing attitude throughout several thousand years of Old Testament history was that to see God was to *die*. (Once more, because God is holy and they were not.)

The Apostle Peter's mother-in-law had previously been healed by Jesus (see Luke 4:38-39), and Peter no doubt was present at the very first miracle—the spellbinding transforming of water into wine at the wedding feast of Cana (John 2:1-11). Yet it was still very early on in Jesus's ministry when Peter witnessed a totally inexplicable miracle (see Luke 5:1-7) involving Peter's personal livelihood of fishing. Right away, Peter had an entirely similar reaction to the afore described Old Testament consequence of utter *dread* in the presence of God.

Overwhelmed, humbled, most of all *terrified* (we know this by Jesus's response to Simon: "Don't be afraid"), Simon Peter said, "Go away from me, Lord; I am a sinful man!" (Luke 5:8). Peter would have had no such reaction had he been "pure in heart." And neither shall we. We are *welcomed*—hurriedly ushered—into the presence of His radiant buoyant face when, like Him (and according to our text today) we are *pure in heart*.

King David, the Psalmist, said "And I—in righteousness I will *see your face*; when I awake, I will be satisfied with seeing your likeness" (Psalm 17:15). He acknowledged the only way he would see God's face was in his own "righteousness," by his own "pure in heart" standing. And when that was the case, he would awaken to the satisfaction of seeing God's "likeness," in his own godly integrity of character.

Let us pray: Lord God, I want to see you in Heaven, but also now! Any one of us, like the Apostle Peter, in mingled humility and fear at your greatness, could say, "Go away from me, Lord; I am a sinful man!" But you stay and lovingly say, "Don't be afraid." Help me and my brothers to be pure in heart. And, Lord, we so desperately want *others* to see you in *our lives*, in our own *Christlike* behavior; in our own "pure in heart" character—then we too shall be "satisfied with seeing your likeness." In your name, Amen.

---

1. What promise does Jesus give to those who are pure in heart?

2. What are some of the revolutionary concepts that were taught by Jesus in the Beatitudes?

3. Why were the ancients afraid to see God?

4. According to David, what is a prerequisite to seeing God's face?

5. Are you seeking purity of heart today?

Day 17

"Although they claimed to be wise, they became fools and exchanged the glory of the immortal God for images made to look like mortal man.... They exchanged the truth of God for a lie, and worshiped and served created things rather than the Creator—who is forever praised. Amen" (Romans 1:22 and 25).

There are few things more foolish than irrevocably exchanging one's precious birthright for a bowl of porridge as Esau did (see Genesis 25:24-34). Yet when a Christian man is lulled and lured into the snare of impure images, he is doing something worse—exchanging the glory of the immortal God "*for images*" and bargaining away the truth of God "*for a lie*."

In the case of Esau, one is voluntarily sacrificing a temporal privilege (a birthright) and human glory so to speak; in the case of our beholding sexual imagery, it is handing over something far more precious—the "truth of God" and the "glory of the immortal God"—not to mention trifling with one's *spiritual* birthright.

It's kind of fascinating when we consider that it has been nearly two thousand years since the Bible's unmitigated condemnation of idol worship involving "images" has had such modern-day relevancy. The ancients would carve or hammer out images in timber and stone, bronze, silver and gold, all in the hope that paying it some kind of homage would materially improve their lives. Tragically, even *God's people*—the people of Israel—were often coaxed into this demonic, worthless enterprise.

After only a few centuries of the Christian Church's advance, the archaic idolatry of bowing down to blocks of wood, stone, or metal greatly diminished, and now has become virtually imperceptible to modern society. Isn't it ironic, then, that with the advent of printing, then photography, then motion pictures, then television, and now the Internet, the human spirit has *devolved* to the point that the dire biblical warnings regarding "images" has once again taken on such relevancy for modern man?

The writer of Psalm 115:4-9 exposed the folly and futility of turning to images for support this way: "But their idols are silver and gold, made by the hands of men. They have mouths, but cannot speak, eyes, but they cannot see; they have ears, but can not hear, noses, but they cannot smell; they have hands, but cannot feel, feet, but they cannot walk; nor can they utter a sound with their throats. Those who make them will be like them, and so will all who trust in them. O house of Israel, trust in the LORD—he is their help and shield."

Today's pornographic images, likewise, have no actual life in them—no breath, no sight, no hearing, no touch or sense of smell. And *neither shall we* if we indulge in them!

The warning is unambiguous: Those who trust in them *will be like them* (Psalm 115:8). To be like them is to be unable to speak, to see, to hear, to feel. It is to be *without senses*—to be *lifeless*. Brothers, obviously we do not want to be lifeless, without senses—at best to become "fools" (Romans 1:22).

None of us would *ever* want to exchange the glory of the immortal God "*for images*" fashioned to look like a mortal (woman). We don't want to exchange the truth of God "*for a lie*." We are being lied to when led to believe that there is satisfaction, fulfillment, and enjoyment (without disastrous consequence) indulging in these images.

The writer of Psalm 115 made his impassioned plea: "O house of Israel, trust in the LORD—he is their help and shield." And *I will make mine*: O house of Jesus, trust in the LORD—*He* is our help and shield!

---

1. For what did the people in Romans 1 exchange the glory of God? For what did they exchange the truth of God?

2. How does "idol worship" apply to people today?

3. What is the result of idolatry in our lives?

4. Do you trust in the Lord? Why should you do so?

DAY 18

"If I had cherished sin in my heart, the Lord would not have listened; but God has surely listened and heard my voice in prayer" (Psalm 66:18-19).

What is the Christian life if *prayer* is eliminated? Or while still prayerful it is rendered meaningless, ineffectual, pointless? Prayer is our most indispensable implement for connecting with our Maker. Praise and worship is our highest expression of love *to* God, Bible instruction our highest enlightenment *from* God, service and love to others our highest expression *of* God, but the benefit to all of these hinge on prayer—our highest intimacy *with* God.

Humble, sincere, consistent prayer is how we enter into social, personal, intimate dialogue and communion with the Creator of the entire cosmos; with the Creator of matter and space and time—the very Savior of our souls. Is it too amazing and thrilling to be true, that this is even possible? Yet *it is true*! Righteous Job referred to "God's intimate friendship" in Job 29:4. That is worth our strenuously striving after and experiencing, Brothers—that each one of us would enjoy *intimate friendship with God.*

"Come near to God and he will come near to you" (James 4:8); "by prayer and petition, with thanksgiving, present your requests to God" (Philippians 4:6); "And I will do whatever you ask in my name, so that the Son may bring glory to the Father" (John 14:13); "Before a word is on my tongue you know it completely, O LORD.... Such knowledge is *too wonderful for me*, too lofty for me to attain" (Psalm 139:4-6).

As Christian men, we must do anything and everything in our power to ensure that nothing disrupts or dilutes our prayers. Romans 3:23 teaches us that "all have sinned and fall short of the glory of God" (also see Proverbs 20:9, Ecclesiastes 7:20, James 2:10). Since we all fall short (repeatedly), then the operative word in today's devotional is "cherished."

Is there any sin of impurity, Brothers, you are *holding onto*? Peer into your hearts for a moment and take closer inventory of what God sees in there and ask yourselves: Is there any area of impurity you are reluctant to let go of?

Is there any DVD with scenes of impurity you are unwilling to toss out, any unrighteous magazines stashed away in your truck or garage or secret drawer? Is there any *mental fantasy* of some woman (in your past, in your everyday life, or perhaps some celebrity) you keep going back to in your mind? Is there anything saved on your computer's hard drive that beckons you into sin periodically? Only you and God know it's there. ["Nothing in all creation is hidden from God's sight. Everything is uncovered and laid bare before the eyes of Him to whom we must give account" (Hebrews 4:13).] You know it should go; you know it's done your soul not an ounce of good, but you've not been ready or able to get rid of it.

These are examples of sins that have become "cherished" in your heart. Today is the day with the forgiveness, power, hope, and help of the Holy Spirit to *stop cherishing* it! Today is the day to stop going back to it; in fact, to *permanently* once and for all remove and destroy it if it exists in any physical form. Today you *are* finally ready and able! Do it at once, my friend!

Proverbs 28:9 says, "If anyone turns a deaf ear to the law, even his prayers are detestable." We can't go a stone's throw further in our Christian walk, Men, if our prayers are detestable to God. Jesus died for us so that the barrier between us and the Holy Father God is now removed. That we would daily enter into God's presence with "confidence," set free from sin, able "to receive mercy," and that God would "help us in our time of need" (Hebrews 4:16) in response to our daily prayers.

If we are married and holding onto any area of impurity, the Word of God informs us we have *especially* hindered our prayers: "Husbands, in the same way be considerate as you live with your wives, and treat them with respect … *so that nothing will hinder your prayers*" (1 Peter 3:7).

To my married brothers: How can we be treating our wives "with respect" if we are sinning against them (whether they know it or not) in areas of sexual impurity? And if we are not respecting them, it is assured that our prayers are undermined.

Let us pray: Father God, we know that if our prayers are hindered, detestable, or worst of all *unlistened to*, we have broken trust with you and have broken off priceless fellowship with you. Please forgive us for those times, restore us to righteousness and strength. For those of us married, keep us always respectful to our wives. Married or single, may we never cherish sin that we could always (like the Psalmist in our lesson) be able to say: "but God *has surely listened* and heard my voice in prayer." In Christ's name, Amen.

---

1. What will prevent God from listening to our prayers?

2. What is your most indispensable implement for connecting with your Master?

3. Is there any sin of impurity that you are holding onto?

4. Do you cherish anything in your mind and/or imagination that you know should not be there?

5. What makes one's prayers "detestable" in God's sight?

6. When you are able to enter God's presence with confidence, what will happen to you?

Day 19

"The eye is the lamp of the body. If your eyes are good, your whole body will be full of light. But if your eyes are bad, your whole body will be full of darkness. If then the light within you is darkness, how great is that darkness!" (Matthew 6:22-23).

On the surface Jesus is talking about something that is very obvious—that eyes bring light to the body, and that if the eyes are bad then naturally the whole body is full of darkness; and the person becomes totally incapable of seeing. In another reference to how obviously vital unimpaired vision is, Jesus says, "If a blind man leads a blind man, both will fall into a pit" (Matthew 15:14).

To think of the eyes as "bad" at first blush reading here is to think of eyes that are damaged, dimmed, or shuttered in such a way as to reduce visibility to utter blindness. That's a very unpleasant thought. The trouble is, Jesus's hearers (as well as each of us) kind of already knew this. Doesn't just about everyone know that if the eyes are bad enough to cause blindness or at least seriously reduce vision, then life is extremely difficult and restricted—that this is a tragic and terrible consequence? As Jesus said, "How great is that darkness!"

So why is he telling us this? Did you ever notice that Jesus never gave a bleak despairing assessment without also presenting *something* within our control to *prevent* the sad, sorry, consequence? That is no less the case in this instance.

When we understand that the word "bad" here is best understood (more literally translated) as "evil," then we understand that Jesus was not talking about an impaired organ concerning visual sight but was explaining what occurs when our eyes are guided by an impaired *heart*, which we otherwise depend upon for *spiritual* sight.

How else could an eye be evil? An eye could no more be evil than a foot or an elbow—two appendages that have neither intrinsic good nor intrinsic badness unto themselves, but must be steered and controlled in order to affect either helpfulness or havoc in our lives. Likewise we steer, control, and *direct* our eyes. And *how* we direct them, Jesus taught here, will affect whether we have shining light or deepest darkness within us.

Proverbs 17:24 says, "A discerning man keeps wisdom in view, but a fool's eyes wander to the ends of the earth." How led astray we can be at times by these portals to both the outside world—where the panorama of color, shape, dimension and texture are observed—and portals to our private *inner* world of imagination, desire, passion and determination.

In 2 Samuel 11:2, King David (unintentionally initially) observed Bathsheba bathing. She was beautiful, according to the story, and from that moment on the results of his inquiry confirming that Bathsheba was *married* (to one of David's own loyal foot soldiers, no less) was irrelevant to David. *Nothing* mattered compared with satisfying the goal of what his eyes had taken mental snapshot of and now were in lusty pursuit of.

The powerful pull of temptation for Eve (at the inception of sin for all mankind in Genesis 3:1-7) wooing her toward that which God had expressly forbidden took hold when Eve *saw* that the fruit:

A) Was "good for food"

B) Was "pleasing to the eye"

C) Was "desirable for gaining wisdom."

It's interesting that the second one (that it "was pleasing to the eye") is first ascribed to a *woman*, when it has been tripping up us *men* ever since far, far more; *we* are the ones repeatedly most often drawn to what is "pleasing to the eye." Like King David, Esau, and countless other men, we are nearly willing to hand over our very souls if not jarred out of sin's eye-appealing intoxication and grip! Let us, therefore, Men, be *wise* with our eyes, recognizing that when our eyes are evil we are full of darkness, but when our eyes are good we shall not stumble, for we are "full of light!"

---

1. What is the "lamp" of your body?

2. What does a "discerning man" always keep in view?

3. Are you a discerning man?

4. What caused Eve to desire the fruit of the Tree of the Knowledge of Good and Evil?

5. What happens when our "eyes" are evil? What happens when our "eyes" are good and wise?

Day 20

"Therefore confess your sins to each other and pray for each other so that you may be healed. The prayer of a righteous man is powerful and effective" (James 5:16).

There are three kinds of confessions:

1) Confessions to God, as the One all sin first and foremost is egregious toward (see 2 Samuel 24:10, Nehemiah 1:6, Luke 15:18, Matthew 6:12, Psalm 38:18, Psalm 41:4, Psalm 51:4, and Proverbs 28:13).

2) Confessions to the person we have directly sinned against (see Exodus 10:16; 1 Samuel 15:24-25, Luke 15:21, and Luke 17:3).

3) And, lastly, confessions to a third-party (an *intercessor,* if you will), a trusted spiritual brother in Christ; perhaps a pastor or priest (see 2 Samuel 12:13, Mark 1:5, and Acts 8:24).

This third form is the confession James is instructing us here to have as a regular regime in our Christian faith walk. James expects us in this instance to seek out a person who is not the one you have sinned against, but rather a person who will receive you with compassion, humility, wisdom, and faith in order that he would be willing and best prepared to pray for you.

This is the kind of non-judgmental person the Apostle Paul refers to who would "restore [you] gently," humble in his own self-awareness that he too might be tempted in the *very same way* were he not ever watchful (Galatians 6:1). We're talking about a man to whom you would not be too embarrassed to confess persistent lust or any other sexual sin.

This is a friend in whom you have established some *mutual* accountability. Confessing to your pastor or priest is advisable, of great benefit, and precisely whom James was thinking of (see 5:14 for this context). However, in our current circumstance, there may be greater benefit to merely seeking out a close Christian brother or two. That is because in addition to our confession, James's instructions include "and pray for each other." Christians certainly should pray for their elders, pastor, or priest, and these servant-leaders for us; but what we are exploring together here is a relationship where the confession and prayer support is a *two-way* street—something that seldom occurs between clergy and their flock.

This is confession and prayer that pertains to serious failures, chronic sinful thoughts, and behavior that warrant James saying "so that you may be *healed*." James was convinced that healing in our body was directly affected, or worse yet left unaffected, by our good standing (clear or marred conscience) before God.

Perhaps the Apostle Paul had personally taught him (or taught Peter who then taught James) this link. Paul was the one who insisted that believers "examine" themselves (see 1

Corinthians 11:28) lest they partake in the Lord's Supper in an unworthy manner. He went so far as to conclude for those who disregarded this important step: "That is why many among you are weak and sick, and a number of you have fallen asleep" (verse 30).

I am certain that James, likewise, had the good intention that no impediment to one's physical wellbeing should ever persist in deference to hanging on to some unconfessed sin. For our sake, I am convinced that keeping a sin unconfessed can be just as much an obstacle to being set free ("healed") from the sin itself!

We don't need to be "healed" of the sin of driving too fast when running late to an appointment. We don't need to be healed of daydreaming during Sunday morning sermons. (On second thought, maybe we do in that regard—bad example.) Nonetheless, where unrelenting, debilitating, lustful thinking and behavior have forged a stronghold in one's life, merely determining to *try harder* is rarely going to produce the desired result; *healing from the Lord Jesus* is what's required.

James advocated that this prayer-accountability partner be a person of personal righteousness. It only makes sense. We need an advocate who is well received at the Father's throne and is one who *believes* that he'll receive what he asks for on our behalf! That is why James said in the same breath, "The prayer of a *righteous man* is powerful and effective."

This is the kind of person who is willing to participate with you in the faithful and committed way that *mutually* you would fulfill Paul's admonition: "Carry each other's burdens, and in this way you will fulfill the law of Christ" (Galatians 6:2). This is a person who sees you regularly in order to know the pulse and pace of your Christian walk in the *best of times* and is therefore at-the-ready (only a phone call or e-mail away) to spring into action with prayer and support on a moment's notice in the *worst of times*.

I have been incalculably grateful that I have a few such good men in my life for accountability and have had so for my entire Christian walk, which started at age fourteen. I know they would view me in the same light regarding their lives, praise God!

The alternative to living a life of regular confession and accountability is keeping one's hidden sin life just that—*hidden*—and living a lie, a life of deception. It is in those private, dimly lit places and choices that Satan reigns; and God's loving mercy and deliverance (the very thing the one with the sin stronghold needs most) is perpetually kept at arms length. "He who conceals his sins does not prosper, but whoever confesses and renounces them finds mercy" (Proverbs 28:13).

I pray that you might have the friend(s) who meet these qualifications, and that you in turn would be such a brother to them—that you would have the *courage* to be transparent with them, unashamed and unafraid of condemnation or rejection. I pray that you would confess to them as often as needed and helpful in the area of male mental moral purity—that you might be *healed*.

---

1. How does the Bible describe the prayer of a righteous man?

2. What are the three kinds of confessions that are discussed in this devotion?

3. Do you have a prayer partner/confidant/friend/Christian brother to whom you can confess your sins?

4. What happens when we confess our moral failings and weaknesses to another believer?

5. How do we fulfill the law of Christ?

6. What is the alternative to living a life of regular confession and accountability?

DAY 21

"Fear God and keep his commandments, for this is the whole duty of man" (Ecclesiastes 12:13).

As evangelical Christians, nearly all of us have come to faith in Christ through some compelling presentation of God's *love*, not his wrath. Since we were drawn close to His side by the heartstrings of mercy, forgiveness, tenderness, and compassion, it feels counterintuitive to "fear" Him. Still, the Bible has an awful lot to say on the subject of fearing God (Proverbs 9:10, Psalm 112:1, and Psalm 25:12 are a small sampling). I think if we are honest with ourselves it makes perfect sense. Here's why.

The Apostle Paul had no doubt in his mind the Roman church would know perfectly well what it meant to fear *human, civil* authorities. So he took a few moments to strongly urge the church to at all times stay on the smart side of the strong arm of the law, stating, "For rulers hold no terror for those who do right, but for those who do wrong" (Romans 13:3a).

He continued from there with the most logical of questions and advice: "Do you want to be free from fear of the one in authority? *Then do what is right* and he will commend you" (Romans 13:3b). Finally Paul concluded with this strongest of warnings: "But if you do wrong, *be afraid*, for he does not bear the sword for nothing."

Like our Roman kinsmen of many centuries ago, twenty-first century Christians are fully up to speed on the benefits of obeying the civil laws, as well as the risks to flaunting them. We get it. As my wife astutely once pointed out, even the serial killer (strange as it may seem) is stopping for red traffic lights on his way to do the killings!

So why are we less apt to fully comprehend the benefits to obeying and risks to disobeying *God's* laws? Psalm 19:11 reads: "By them [the ordinances of the Lord] is your servant warned; in keeping them there is great reward." How is it we can view God's laws as less important, less inconvertible, less correct and laudable than the human laws to which we readily toe the line? Have we concluded that God is less concerned, less vigilant than the human civil law enforcers to see that *His* laws are respected and upheld?

The Bible is adamant that our "God is a consuming fire" (Hebrews 12:29)—One who "expresses his wrath every day" (Psalm 7:11) and disciplines those whom He loves (Hebrews 12:6). It may be a totally new idea for some of you, but God is actually *content* to have us fear him—provided it motivates us to make the right choices, the best choices for our lives and regarding those we impact around us. God loves us, and our most righteous (and therefore *best possible*) life is His ultimate intention.

By the way, this isn't a compromise or exchange for God's mercy and forgiveness. Knowing, receiving, and relishing in God's love *is compatible* with fearing Him. And that is how

God *wants* it. It's worth repeating: the Lord disciplines those He loves. "We have all had human fathers who disciplined us and we respected them for it. How much more should we submit to the Father of our spirits and live!" (Hebrews 12:9).

The good news is that as we incorporate this truth, it actually keeps us from running afoul. It promotes discipline and purity in us—the very things we're seeking after—in order to please God and have the best lives possible. Proverbs 16:6b fully sums this up: "Through the fear of the LORD a man avoids evil." Similarly, "A wise man fears the LORD and shuns evil" (Proverbs 14:16).

In 1 Corinthians 10:8, the Apostle Paul said, "We should not commit sexual immorality, as some of them did—and in one day twenty-three thousand of them died." Paul was referring to an Old Testament event and severity of judgment that, thankfully, we have not seen the likes of since. Nonetheless, Paul was warning *New* Testament believers, "These things happened to them as examples and were written down as *warnings for us*" (1 Corinthians 10:11).

Paul reminded them of such a dreadful event because he wanted sexual immorality to stop being so accommodated and tolerated in the Corinthian church. Paul was not telling them (nor is the Holy Spirit telling us today) that they would be struck dead for sexual improprieties. Were that the case, the Church would nearly cease to exist. Rather, He was using this graphic example in effect to say, "Stop taking this matter lightly! Fear God! Clean up your act!"

He was reminding them of the goal our text for today says: "*Keep his commandments.*" For as Hebrews 10:31

(another *New* Testament passage) warns us, "It is a dreadful thing to fall into the hands of the living God."

---

1. What, according to Ecclesiastes 12:13, is the whole duty of man?

2. What drew you to Jesus in the first place?

3. What will keep you from "running afoul"?

4. According to Proverbs 16:6, how can you avoid evil.

Day 22

"Flee from sexual immorality. All other sins a man commits are outside his body, but he who sins sexually sins against his own body" (1 Corinthians 6:18).

Experts in the field of psychology determined many years ago that when a human being is in a situation of recognizable imminent danger, his body will have a fight-or-flight response. In other words, *fight back* or *get away!* The behavioral scientists believe a rational sizing up of the threat and weighing one's reasonable chance for success is not what happens initially, but instead an instantaneous response of the autonomic nervous system of fight or flight. A racing heartbeat or involuntarily screaming would be examples of this that commonly occur when a person is suddenly facing great peril.

According to God's Word, in the area of sexual sin *we are the threat to ourselves!* With the great advantage of spiritual insight versus a behavioral sciences theorem, the Apostle Paul chose *flight* over fight, urging us to "flee from sexual immorality." When it comes to sexual temptation, our personal well-being is in mortal danger; so in automatic, urgent, involuntary response, we are told here to *escape!*

In reality, having the benefit of time in most instances to assess the threat when tempted with impure thoughts and sexual sins, we can legitimately ask ourselves, "Since I am going to *harm myself* by these sexual thoughts or actions, why proceed any further?"

When Paul commended husbands to love their wives "as their own bodies" (Ephesians 5:28-29), he explained that "After all, no one ever hated his own body, but he feeds it and cares for it, just as Christ does the church." There is a great irony, therefore, when we give in to sexual sins. We do so in an attempt to *care for own body*, yet the Word of God here repudiates that by declaring, "He who sins sexually *sins against his own body.*" We are in fact *not caring* for our own bodies at those times but *harming ourselves*.

Similarly, Proverbs 6:32 teaches us that "a man who commits adultery lacks judgment; whoever does so *destroys himself.*" Since Christ has warned us that to look lustfully upon a woman is to commit adultery in one's heart (Matthew 5:27-28), we are even in those cases little by little chipping away at our inner man, degrading our souls, *destroying* ourselves.

Following Christ is sometimes like living in an alternate reality. It is a matter of choosing to follow the truth even when our physical senses or mental faculties tell us otherwise. Proverbs 3:5 is perhaps the best Old Testament precursor to this principle when it says: "Trust in the LORD with all your heart and *lean not on your own understanding.*" Another Old Testament example of this is found in Proverbs 14:12, which states: “There is a way that *seems right to a man*, but in the end it leads to death.”

Jesus Christ constantly challenged His disciples in these paradoxical ways. Consider this smattering of samples: “The man who loves his life will lose it, while the man who hates his life in this world will keep it for eternal life” (John 12:25). “The Spirit gives life; the flesh counts for nothing” (John 6:63). “Whoever finds his life will lose it, and whoever loses his life for my sake will find it” (Matthew 10:39). “But seek first his kingdom and his righteousness; and all these things [regarding food and drink and clothing—bodily provisions] will be given to you as well” (Matthew 6:33).

I’m sure Jesus’s disciples had a lot of furrowed brows and befuddled looks on their faces as Jesus was teaching them these things. They had so much that needed to be *unlearned* as a matter of first course in order to absorb these truths of vibrant kingdom, Christ-follower living.

As contemporary disciples of Jesus Christ, we, too, must *unlearn* many of our natural inclinations—how we care for our own bodies in ways that seem most satisfying and expedient. We need to believe once and for all that fulfilling our sexual impulses in *any* impure, unrighteous manner at all is *detrimental* to our well-being and tantamount to hating ourselves!

Proverbs 3:7-8 states, “Do not be wise in your own eyes; fear the LORD and shun evil. *This* will bring health to your body and nourishment to your bones.” That includes our sexual health and contentment. Bring about no harm to yourself this day, my Brothers!

---

1. Why should you flee from sexual immorality?

2. What does one sin against when he engages in sexual immorality?

3. What will bring health to your body and nourishment to your bones?

Day 23

"The thief comes only to steal and kill and destroy; I have come that they may have life, and have it to the full" (John 10:10).

Closing in on four decades of personally following the Good Shepherd of John 10, I have not yet heard a preacher of God's Word refer to John 10:10 without swiftly declaring that it is the devil (Satan) who is the thief who comes to "steal and kill and destroy." This virtually universal interpretation is curious to me, for nowhere in the text does Jesus express or for that matter really even imply that it is the devil He is speaking of.

Instead, from the chapter's very first verse Jesus starts off His searing indictment of the "thief" by speaking merely of the "one" (Greek transliteration), while the pronoun "he" is employed in the King James Version, and the word "man" is transposed into the text by the New International Version translators. Additionally, in each of the translations Jesus extended His condemnation to *plural* "thieves" (John 10:8), making it eminently clear that He was not referring to Satan.

For our devotional considerations, this is important because not every temptation—moral, spiritual, and societal destruction—is wrought upon the world by Satan. The world is abounding with evil *men* (and evil women), and for every evil person there are twice as many who are at minimum misguided.

Surely Satan is pleased and complicit in their misdeeds; but, unlike God, the devil isn't omnipresent. When the devil "entered" Judas in John 13:27, for instance, he wasn't also giving his demon army its evening revelry. When he petitioned God for permission to "sift" Simon Peter like wheat (see Luke 22:31), he wasn't simultaneously devising up new strategies for the corruption of humanity. There is much more daily temptation and havoc thrust upon us from our own sinful inclinations and from other fallen human beings around us than Satan alone can personally inflict.

Still, with agents of spiritual and moral theft, murder, and destruction (intent to "steal and kill and destroy") lurking at every corner, Jesus offered us the only antiserum—*Zoë* (pronounced "*Zoh*-ay"); the life only found in God. "I have come that they may have life [*Zoë*], and have it to the full," Jesus triumphantly announced.

The language of ancient Greece (so much richer than ours) had three words that we English-speaking persons merely translate as *life*. *Bios*, the first of these, represented the *biological* life in all living matter, both in human and plant life. Next, *Psyche* (pronounced Psoo-*kay*") is the *psychological* life that exists in a person, yet not within the pine cone. And last of all, *Zoë* is the *spiritual* life only found in God and then is imparted to believers as a gift from God—evidence of the *presence of the living God* living within us!

It is the irrefutable, irrevocable life in the Spirit that Jesus offers each and every repentant, open heart to Him (see John 3:5-6).

Zoë is what the Apostle Paul wonderfully referred to as "*the life that is truly life*" (1 Timothy 6:19). *This*, my Friends, is the "life" Jesus speaks of when he says, "I have come that they may have *Zoë*, and have it to the full!"

When we are tempted, Brothers, we need to pull out our *Zoë* dipstick to see how "full" the life of God is within us, for Jesus says ardently that He wants us to "have it *to the full*." When our *Zoë* is not to the full line, we are wide open to give in to temptation we otherwise would have no interest in. We are vulnerable because we are not full up, in and with, the *Zoë* life in the Spirit!

Jesus told the (*Zoë*-less) Samaritan woman at the well, "Everyone who drinks this water will be thirsty again, but whoever drinks the water I give him will never thirst" (John 4:13-14).

She was clueless to the fact that Jesus was talking about a *spiritual* refreshment, something no well on earth could supply. That was why she responded quite naturally, "Sir, give me this drink so that I won't get thirsty and have to keep coming here to draw water" (verse 15).

Brothers, we have received the new drink from the Lord's own ladle! We have within each one of us the "spring of water welling up to eternal life" (John 4:14)—*living water* as it were (see John 4:10 and 7:38). So why don't we act like it? Why would we ever continue to live and act as if we were as parched and empty as this woman presently on her sixth lover? In truth, when we look upon a woman impurely, aren't we on our one thousand and sixth lover?

"As the deer pants for streams of water, so my soul pants for you, O God. My soul thirsts for God, for the living God. When can I go and meet God?" (Psalm 42:1-2). These words were expressed by a man like you and me—a man who *yearned* for God—with one exception: The psalmist did not have the "living water," the quenching Holy Spirit, interacting with his own spirit in the way we do (see John 16:7 and 20:21-22, Acts 1:4-5, Joel 2:28-29, John 4:10). *Our thirst should never approximate his!*

Do you need *Zoë* to the full ("*abundantly*" in the KJV) this day, Friends? For any one of us, if this is so, here is what we must ask: *When can I go and meet with God?* How soon can I get alone with Him in my prayer closet? How soon can I spend priority, uninterrupted time reading and meditating upon His Holy Word? How soon can I go and worship Him in the presence and camaraderie of His Son's living body, the Church?

"Whom have I in heaven but you? And earth has nothing I desire besides you" (Psalm 73:25). The disciple Peter echoed this so perfectly: "Lord to whom shall we go? You have the words of eternal life. We believe and know that you are the Holy One of God" (John 6:68-69).

Let us pray: Father God, help us find and always remember our sole sufficiency in you. You not only bring us the words of life, you give us life—*Zoë*, spiritual life itself, and as *living water* within us we need not ever thirst again. Help us not only to believe this in our minds, but receive and recognize this daily in our souls, that we would never seek to be filled with any thing impure, which can never quench our spirit's thirst as you alone can. In Christ's name, Amen.

---

1. According to John 10:10, why did Jesus come?

2. Is Jesus referring to Satan as a thief in the above verse?

3. What are the three Greek words for "life"? What does each one mean?

4. Are you walking in abundant life?

5. Do you regularly get alone with God in your "prayer closet"?

6. Do you attend church regularly?

Day 24

"But among you there must not be even a hint of sexual immorality, or any kind of impurity.... Have nothing to do with the fruitless deeds of darkness, but rather expose them" (Ephesians 5:3 and 11).

When you think of the Church and some of its most prominent leaders on a nationwide basis, do you think of an institution and body of people that has been free of "even a *hint* of sexual immorality?"

When you think of the church you presently attend, and include the ones you've attended in the past, do you think of a church and fellowship of believers that has been free of "even a *hint* of sexual immorality?"

When you think of your best and closest Christian friends, do you think of a sampling of marriages and specific individuals who have been "free of even a *hint* of sexual immorality?"

When you think of your own life (particularly the life that only you and God see), do you think of a man who's blameless of "even a *hint* of sexual immorality?"

The Apostle Paul was a man like you and me. He was far from perfect. While he clearly is inspirational to us in issues of abstinence and personal purity matters, he evidently had a temper and impatience about certain persons that I don't seek to emulate. Go and review Galatians 5:12, Titus 1:12, or 2 Timothy 4:14 the next time you're short or unkind with someone you care about; and you may feel much better about yourself. (You'll still need to go and apologize, but you may feel less like a *total failure* in your Christianity!)

I say this to remind us that Paul was a man—a regular, red-blooded, Y-chromosome male—and men, as you know, have a hormonal tempest going on much of the time that is barely under control, let alone entirely dominated. Nonetheless, Paul, by the power of the Holy Spirit, knew these impulses *can* be tamed and *must* be tamed if we are going to emulate (in fact *represent*) Jesus Christ accurately and effectively to the world.

First off, we must continually remind ourselves that these deeds are *fruitless*—meaning of *no benefit* to ourselves or anyone else. Jesus Christ has called us to bear fruit (the complete opposite of *fruitless*, by the way). Not only that, but He intends for us to produce *lasting* fruit (see John 15:16). We cannot bear His fruit and have lasting results to God's glory if we are still playing around with fruitless sexual titillations of one kind or another.

We are to have "*nothing to do* with the fruitless deeds of darkness." How can there be so much sexual sin in the Church—in supposedly God-fearing persons—while we are having "nothing to do" with these things? It's as if we don't even take these marks of true discipleship seriously.

We are not only to be personally and collectively exonerated from sexual sins; we are called to "expose them!" (verse 11). And here's the curious thing about that added requirement: it doesn't mean embarrassing people. By exposing them, Paul was not talking about *talking* about them. If that were what Paul meant by *exposing* these sins, he wouldn't have followed up these instructions by immediately *contradicting* himself by saying, "For it is shameful *even to mention* what the disobedient do in secret" (Ephesians 5:12).

What he meant by exposing them was exposing the *deeds* (without pointing fingers) within our fellowships, most of all in our own hearts and minds, for what they are—"fruitless deeds of darkness." Paul was urgently cajoling us out of the darkness (where things are hidden, unexposed) back to where we belong, where everything is *exposed* under the light of Christ. "You were once darkness, but now you are light in the Lord. *Live as children of light*" (Ephesians 5:8).

Of all the many chapters in all his nine books of instruction, encouragement, and rebuke, the Apostle Paul wrote to his Christian charges in the first century churches of Rome, Corinth, Galatia, Ephesus, Philippi, Colossae, and Thessalonica and taking into account all the chapters in his four epistles (personal letters) to Timothy, Titus, and Philemon, this is the only place in which Paul urged his listeners to "find out what pleases the Lord" (verse 10) and "understand what the Lord's will is" (verse 17).

In Romans 12:2, he explained *how* to do this: *"Do not conform* any longer to the pattern of this world, but *be transformed* by the renewing of your mind. *Then* you will be able to test and approve what God's will is—his good, pleasing and perfect will."

We know that lust and sexual immorality—for that matter "*any kind* of impurity" (Ephesians 5:3)—does not please God. To live in the light consists of "goodness, righteousness and truth" (verse 9). That is what we must seek after for ourselves and for one another. That is what will please our Lord and will prepare us for understanding His will for our individual and collective lives. And isn't that the highest objective for our lives, Brothers, to please Him and understand what His will is for us?

---

1. What should you do about the "fruitless works of darkness"?

2. Is there any "hint" of sexual immorality in your life?

3. Review Galatians 5:1, Titus 1:12, and 2 Timothy 4:14. What do these verses say to you?

4. How, according to Romans 12:2, can you avoid conformity to the world and its ways?

5. What is the highest objective for our lives?

Day 25

"Those who live according to the sinful nature have their minds set on what that nature desires; but those who live in accordance with the Spirit have their minds set on what the Spirit desires" (Romans 8:5).

When the great Billy Graham was questioned regarding the nature of lust, he explained, "If you walk down the street and happen to catch a glimpse of an attractive woman coming your way, that's not a sin. It's taking that *second look* that is the sin." This is precisely what the Apostle Paul in today's devotional is referring to—our giving in to lots of *second* looks. It is where your heart "sets" that God is concerned with, not our startled glances and wholesome appreciation of someone's attractiveness.

Paul stated in Galatians 5:17, "The sinful nature desires what is contrary to the Spirit, and the Spirit what is contrary to the sinful nature." My flesh—your flesh—desires things *contrary* to God's best and preferred will for us. Our unspiritual manhood desires money, prestige, physical comforts, sexual gratification. Things in and of themselves that are not evil, but unrestrained, we are prone to strive for without regard for whether they are obtained in a righteous manner, and regardless of whether they glorify God in our lives.

As regenerated men, rather, we are to "look not only to your own interests, but also to the interests of others" (Philippians 2:4). Or, as Paul, quoting the Lord Jesus to the believers of Ephesus, said, "It is more blessed to give than to receive" (Acts 20:35). Lastly, "*Whatever* you do, do it all for the glory of God" (1 Corinthians 10:31). Put simply, put others ahead of yourself as much as possible, and in all things make decisions and take actions with the overarching motive of glorifying the Lord. These are to be our guideposts.

So how do you take a mind set on what the *sinful* nature desires and cooperate or assist in its transformation into a mind set on what the *Spirit* desires? You start off with the humility of conducting a non-defensive, inner self-assessment regarding where your mind sets much of the time regarding godly and *ungodly* thinking. As a man "*thinketh* in his heart, so he is" (Proverbs 23:7, KJV).

If very often your mind is noticeably set on what the sinful nature desires, it's high time to disrupt that comfortable, familiar pattern of thinking. It's overdue to re-familiarize yourself with what *the Spirit desires*; to "fix these words of mine [God's] in your hearts and *minds*" (Deuteronomy 11:18), and to *hold on* to what Jesus has taught us when He said, "If you *hold to my teaching*, you are really my disciples. *Then* you will know the truth, and the truth will set you free" (John 8:31-32).

It is impossible to hold to what Jesus has taught us while simultaneously having our minds clinging onto what the sinful nature desires. Did you hear me? It bears saying this again: *It is impossible to hold to what Jesus has taught us while simultaneously having our minds clinging onto what the sinful nature desires.* If your mind is set on impure thoughts and images, it's time to renew your grip and hold onto the teachings of Christ Jesus. Christ promised that this (the "truth" he has laid out for us) will "set you free" (John 8:32).

Right before the Apostle Paul gave us the thrilling and incomparable nine qualities of the Fruit of the Spirit in Galatians 5:22, he said (for bold *comparison's* sake as much as anything else), "The acts of the sinful nature are obvious" (Galatians 5:19). At the top of the diabolic list are the *two most obvious* acts of the sinful nature—"sexual immorality" and "impurity." It's kind of uncanny in regard to our twenty-first century struggles, don't you think? In stark contrast, Paul then pointed out, "But the fruit of *the Spirit* is love, joy, peace, patience, kindness, goodness, faithfulness, gentleness and self-control" (verses 22-23).

Ephesians 4:22-24 reminds us, "You were taught, with regard to your former way of life, to put off your old self, which is being corrupted by its deceitful desires; *to be made new in the attitude of your minds*; and to put on the new self, *created to be like God* in true righteousness and holiness." Likewise, Paul admonished the church in Romans 12:2, "Do not conform any longer to the pattern of this world, but be *transformed by the renewing of your mind*."

Do you want to have your mind "*set*" on what the "evil nature" desires? Then *live* according to those thought patterns! Do you want to have your mind set on what the Spirit desires? Then "live in accordance with the Spirit" (Romans 8:5); accordingly when you "live by the Spirit … you will not gratify the desires of the sinful nature" (Galatians 5:16).

Once more I ask: Do you genuinely desire to have your mind set on what the Spirit desires? I know that you do, Brothers! Then here is where to center your thoughts: "Whatever is *true*, whatever is *noble*, whatever is *right*, whatever is *pure*, whatever is *lovely*, whatever is *admirable*—if anything is *excellent* or *praiseworthy—think about such things*" (Philippians 4:8).

Let us pray: Father God, we fall at your feet and humbly confess that we need a Holy Spirit extreme mind-makeover. We can not in and of ourselves make new the attitude of our minds. If you don't do it, it won't happen. We determine this day as never before to cooperate with your Spirit in this regard, but we need *him* to make new the attitude in our minds. We need his presence and power, strategy and strength in order to have our minds set on what *your Spirit desires* instead of what our old, stubbornly resilient, sinful nature desires. Help us this day and every day, Lord, to live according to your Spirit. In Christ's name, Amen.

---

1. Are you living in accordance with the Holy Spirit?

2. What did Billy Graham say about taking a "second look" at an attractive woman?

3. How do you transform your mind-set into what the Holy Spirit desires for you?

4. What is the role of truth in your life?

5. What is the fruit of the Holy Spirit?

Day 26

"So if the Son sets you free, you will be free indeed" (John 8:36).

Long before the *Emancipation Proclamation* regarding the freeing of slaves in America, Jesus gave us this *universal* emancipation proclamation: "If the Son sets you free, you will be free indeed." Only moments prior to this, Jesus diagnosed just exactly what it is the human condition needs to be liberated from: "I tell you the truth, everyone who sins is a slave to sin" (John 8:34). Jesus's impetuous yet precious disciple, Peter, reverberated this a few years later when he said, "A man is a slave to *whatever has mastered him*" (2 Peter 2:19).

Slaves are bound by physical or psychological chains of one kind or another, but either way they are controlled and held captive. What Jesus was saying was that if you sin repeatedly (*uncontrollably,* as it were) you are held *captive to sin*. You are in its grip, its power, and, yes, even its *service.* Jesus, on the other hand, offered us our true, legal, and lasting freedom when He proclaimed, "If the Son sets you free, you will be free indeed."

You see, the master of an estate could set a slave free. Yet, if he had a firstborn son, that son might object and seek to revoke the slave's release from bondage. As rightful legal heir to the estate and all of its belongings, he might easily surmise that the slaves were each one his own (*eventually*) and that the father was, in reality, compromising his inheritance by this amnesty.

Therefore, if the *son* set the slave free, there was no one left to repeal the slave's freedom. That is why Jesus said assuredly, "So if the *Son* sets you free, you will be free indeed." We need, each and every one of us, that kind of *irrevocable* freedom from sin's vise grip.

That is what Jesus Christ, and only Jesus Christ, offers us. He is the "only begotten Son," the inheritor of all that is the Father's (see Matthew 21:38). When Christ, therefore, has set us free—*because He is the Son*—we are free indeed!

Christ is not only interested in freeing us from sin's *penalty* (hell) but also sin's *power* over our lives. Since the Son has set us free, if we have become re-entangled in the sins of lust and impurity, it is our own doing!

"Of them the proverbs are true: 'A dog returns to its vomit,' and, 'A sow that is washed goes back to her wallowing in the mud'" (2 Peter 2:22). In which case, the Apostle Peter goes further to say, he is worse off than if he never came to Christian faith in the first place! "If they have escaped the corruption of the world by knowing our Lord and Savior Jesus Christ and are *again entangled in it* and *overcome*, they are worse off at the end than they were at the beginning." (verse 20; when able, see the whole passage of 2 Peter 2:19-22 and Psalm 85:8).

Read Romans 6:22, 1 Corinthians 7:22, Ephesians 6:6, and Romans 6:18, and you will see that the only thing God wants us to be *slaves* to is himself, to Christ, and to "righteousness." By the inner-working, *inner-living* Spirit of the Lord there is freedom (2 Corinthians 3:17). So, Brothers, do not let yourselves be burdened again with a yoke of slavery to sexual sin in *any* of its forms. The Son has set you free! There is no one left to repeal His clemency, and you are free indeed!

1.What is the universal "emancipation proclamation" of Jesus?

2. What kinds of things have the potential to enslave us?

3. From what does Jesus want to free you?

4. Are you free indeed?

Day 27 – Morning

"As obedient children, do not conform to the evil desires you had when you lived in ignorance. But just as he who called you is holy, so be holy in all you do; for it is written: 'Be holy, because I am holy'" (1 Peter 1:14-16).

It would be so wonderfully perfect if the "evil desires" we had when we "lived in ignorance" were never ever experienced again—never repeated in any way, shape, or form—once we turned in faith to Christ. Obviously, were that the case, the Apostle Peter would not have written such indicting words about and for us.

That is not to say that evil desires should be anywhere *near* what they were when we lived in ignorance. Thank God, they are continually being affected, confronted, muted, impounded, and banished by the Holy Spirit within us and by our interaction with God's transforming Holy Word (see Hebrews 4:12). After all, we are "being transformed into his likeness with ever-increasing glory, which comes from the Lord, who is the Spirit" (2 Corinthians 3:18).

We are being *transformed into the likeness of Christ*! That's really such fantastic and remarkable news, but we mustn't forget that it is exactly as it sounds—a *process*. We are "*being* transformed," versus having "*been* transformed." While in the process and progression of being transformed into the likeness of Christ, be fully aware, my Brothers, that echoes, faint traces (occasional fierce eruptions) of evil desires you had when you lived in ignorance may at times reemerge. That is what Peter is concerning us with.

In the pursuit of male mental moral purity, residual impure passions can be anywhere from mildly annoying to utterly devastating. Mild or ferocious, either way, the apostle is unwavering here: "Do not conform to the evil desires."

With God's wisdom, grace, and power within us, we can overcome them. Jesus promised us, "In this world you will have trouble. But take heart! I have overcome the world" (John 16:33). Are you still in the world? Of course you are! Jesus assures you then that you can expect trouble—cartloads of it!

Even so, take heart! Jesus has overcome the world, and now by faith He lives in us. Will your life to be *overtaken* by temptation and evil desires? Or will you *overcome* anything the world, the devil, or the weakened inner man has to throw at you? It's now up to you. Will you be overtaken by temptation this day or will you (by Christ's triumphant Spirit within you) overcome the world?

Day 27 – Evening

"As obedient children, do not conform to the evil desires you had when you lived in ignorance. But just as he who called you is holy, so be holy in all you do; for it is written, 'Be holy, because I am holy'" (1 Peter 1:14-16).

The Apostle Peter was himself *far* from perfect. To this day he is widely remembered for *three times* denying (and within a very short time span) that he even *knew* who Christ was (Matthew 26:69-74); for *boasting* only hours beforehand that even if *all* the other disciples deserted Jesus, he certainly never would (Matthew 26:33); for being *publicly* rebuked by the Apostle Paul (Galatians 2:11-14); and for nearly drowning in utter panic after only moments before (in awe-inspiring faith) walking on the water with Jesus (Matthew 14:30).

He is remembered for his recalcitrant "Surely not, Lord!" (Acts 10:14) when told to kill and eat animals that were previously prohibited meals; for actually *rebuking the Lord* (Mark 8:32) when Jesus spoke of His impending sacrificial death, and for being more or less *disoriented* at the appearance of the glorified Jesus alongside the apparitions of Moses and Elijah (Matthew 17:4).

We remember him for his trying to set a *fixed* number of times one is obligated to forgive someone (Matthew 18:21), for boasting and complaining all in the same breath over how much he and the other disciples had sacrificed for the Lord (Matthew 19:27), and for falling asleep while Jesus prayed and desperately desired Peter's companionship during His solitary long hour of anguish (Matthew 26:40).

He registered the sole protest when Jesus began washing His disciples' feet (John 13:8), and put his outer garment *back on* before jumping into the lake (John 21:7) in his attempt to swim to the risen Lord on shore. (*This was the man* who told us to be "obedient children" and to "be holy in all you do.")

But here equally is the man who spontaneously left his nets (his wage-earning livelihood) in answer to the call to follow the Lord (Matthew 4:18-20), who left his wife for long periods of time in order to be by the Master's side (Luke 18:28-29), who had the imagination and courage to walk on the water with Jesus (Matthew 14:28), and was *first* to realize and say to Jesus, "You are the Christ, the Son of the living God" (Matthew 16:16).

Peter was the one to whom Jesus said, "On this rock I will build my church" (Matthew 16:18), was one of only three of Jesus's *closest* disciples whom Jesus invited into exclusive, extraordinary circumstances (Luke 8:51 and 9:28, Matthew 26:37). Peter was the sole disciple to physically resist Jesus's being arrested (John 18:10); and, though outrun by John to the tomb of Christ, was the braver of the two in entering the tomb despite John's initial timidity (John 20:3-8).

Imbued with the power of the Holy Spirit, Peter was the first to preach and preside over Christianity's first-ever evangelistic crusade (Acts 2:14-41). He was the first follower of Jesus to successfully perform a miraculous healing in Christ's name (Acts 3:1-10), was *unapologetic* in the face of certain incarceration and possible torture and death (Acts 4:19-20), and was fearless (taking on tremendous personal risk) *flagrantly* disregarding direct orders to stop preaching (Acts 5:28-32).

Peter was able to successfully predict sudden imminent death for the wily couple who attempted to deceive the Church and Holy Spirit (Acts 5:1-10); he (quite possibly) caused healing to occur for cripples when his mere *shadow* passed over them (Acts 5:15); and was in faith able to dispense the gift of the Holy Spirit to others by the laying on of hands (Acts 8:15-17). Subsequently, he could not be *bribed* in order to share the Holy Spirit, and was thoroughly outraged at the notion (Acts 8:18-23).

He preached the gospel throughout Samaria, a region that was often very hostile to Jews (Acts 8:25); healed the cripple Aeneas in the name of Jesus Christ (Acts 9:34); and after prayerfully beseeching God from his knees, Peter raised a beloved Christian woman *from the dead* (Acts 9:40). He preached to and baptized the non-Jewish Gentiles before the Apostle Paul ever did (Acts 10:34-48) and was supernaturally rescued from his iron stocks (bound between two guards), then literally ushered out of prison by a walking, living *angel* (Acts 12:6-10).

Peter was the leading apostle to the Jews (Galatians 2:8) and wrote two amazing epistles that still edify us today. Some believe he went on to become the first bishop of Rome. Tradition says he was martyred by crucifixion at the edict of the monstrous Emperor Nero and that Peter himself demanded that he be crucified upside down, feeling unworthy to die in the same right side-up manner as his Lord had been crucified.

In all of this, Peter became our example—Behold, the man who told us to "be obedient children" and to "be holy in *all* you do." Be holy this day, my Brothers!

---

1. You are being transformed into the image of Christ. What does this mean to you?

2. What is holiness? Is it an unattainable goal?

3. Are you living a holy life?

4. How can you prevent your life from being overtaken by temptations and evil desires?

5. Have you chosen to overcome the world and its allurements? How will you be able to do so?

DAY 28

"Therefore, there is now no condemnation for those who are in Christ Jesus" (Romans 8:1).

For the Christian man, struggling with issues of pornography or even persistent lust is thoroughly demoralizing. There are few sins that can throw one's confidently good standing with God into such mental uncertainty. Nagging, troubling doubts about whether God still loves and accepts you are part and parcel with the struggle.

There are thirty other devotionals in the month—each one dedicated to "spur one another on toward love and good deeds" (Hebrews 10:24)—toward greater *righteousness*. This one, however, is strictly dedicated to reinforcing and reminding us of God's unconditional love and forgiveness—His unrelenting acceptance of us. "For as high as the heavens are above the earth, *so great is his love* for those who fear him; as far as the east is from the west, so far has he *removed our transgressions from us*" (Psalm 103:11-12).

Jesus said in Mark 3:28-29, "I tell you the truth, all sins and blasphemes of men will be forgiven them. But whoever blasphemes against the Holy Spirit will never be forgiven;

he is guilty of an eternal sin." What precisely it means to "blaspheme against the Holy Spirit" has been dissected and debated by gaggles of theological minds (far superior to mine) down through the ages. That is not what we're interested in getting at here.

What I want you to zero in on, Brothers, is the stupendous (all at once scintillating while serene) truth that: "*All* sins and blasphemes of men will be forgiven them!"

God forbid that your unbridled sexual impulses have already led to the breakup of a marriage or two in your life. How unfortunate and avoidable that would be. Even *that* can be forgiven. Divorce is not the unforgivable sin; it is not blasphemy against the Holy Spirit. *Every single one* of your sins involving sexuality is forgivable.

That is, after all, why Jesus died for us—to take away the sins of the world (see John 1:29). "For God did not send his Son into the world to condemn the world, but to save the world through him" (John 3:17). The Apostle Paul put it this concisely: "I do not set aside the grace of God, for if righteousness could be obtained through the law [that is, perfectly performing the do's and don'ts of the Torah, God's commandments] Christ died for nothing!" (Galatians 2:21).

"Very rarely will anyone die for a righteous man, though for a good man someone might possibly dare to die. But God demonstrates his own love for us in this: While we were still sinners, Christ died for us. Since we have now been justified by his blood, how much more shall we be saved from God's wrath through him!" (Romans 5:7-9).

Love "keeps no record of wrongs" (1 Corinthians 13:5). That includes, Brothers, our keeping active reminders *unto ourselves* of *our own* sins. To continue to do so is to not love *oneself*, which is in direct opposition to what Jesus wanted for us when He taught, "Love your neighbor *as yourself*" (Mark 12:31). What we instead need to constantly remind ourselves of is this: "Whoever comes to me I will never drive away" (John 6:37).

"Because of the Lord's great love we are not consumed, for his compassions never fail. They are *new every morning*; great is your faithfulness" (Lamentations 3:22-23). And "if we confess our sins, he [Jesus] is faithful and just and *will forgive us our sins* and purify us from all unrighteousness" (1 John 1:9). Did you catch that? He not only forgives us, but as we come to Him in humility and confession, He continually *purifies* us. He *forgives* and *renews* us!

"So from now on we regard no one [*not even our own selves*] from a worldly point of view.... Therefore, if anyone is in Christ, he is *a new creation*; the old has gone, the new has come!" (2 Corinthians 5:16-17). Do you feel like a new creation this day, Brother? It's true, you are one! The old is dead and gone. Rejoice!

Let us pray: Once again, thank you *so much*, Father God, for Jesus's dying on our behalf. Thank you that your compassions are new *every* morning. The old is dead and gone; and, behold, we are new! Thank you for loving us while we were yet sinners, and now, as your beloved sanctified children, loving us all the more! Thank you for never giving up on us, no matter how many times we fail you; that you will *never* drive us away. Thank you that you not only forgive us but continually purify us. We happily receive your love. We love you back, *Abba* Father God. In Christ's name, Amen.

---

1. Does God forgive sexual sins?

2. Why did God send His Son into the world?

3. What justifies us in the sight of God?

4. What does Jesus do when we confess our sins to Him?

5. Do you feel like a new creation in Christ Jesus? Why, or why not?

6. Have you confessed your sins to the Lord?

Day 29

"Why embrace the bosom of another man's wife? For a man's ways are in full view of the LORD, and he examines all his paths" (Proverbs 5:20-21).

King Solomon originally prescribed these provocative words when there were no televisions, no movies, and no Internet. Solomon nonetheless keenly understood how the male's rapt attention to the female's curvaceous anatomy would represent the precursor to a great many sins.

Nowadays, scantily-clad, buxom, gaping-cleavage women are unashamedly emphasized in (what certainly seems like) half of the commercials on television—selling beer, cars, perfumes, the latest motion picture advertisement, woman's underclothes (of course), and so forth, not to mention the *actual* TV shows and movies we have to select from. It's a national obsession of sorts. My wife has said on more than one occasion, "Hollywood has no mercy on us wives!"

As we've already fully established, Jesus viewed lusting in one's heart for a woman with some equivalence to committing sex with her (Matthew 5:27-28). Consequently, Solomon posed a very current question to us: Why embrace (even figurative-speaking, visually, or mentally versus *literally*) the bosom of another man's wife? Why do it?

Sometimes the little conjunction words (such as and or but) in the Bible are actually the product-key to discovering the message God is trying to get across. Today's passage is one of those instances. Right after the provocative, piercing, question we are considering—"Why embrace the bosom of another man's wife?"—Solomon used the conjunction "for," and it enables us to apprehend exactly what we need to walk away with here.

"Why embrace the bosom of another man's wife? *For* [when, whereby, or in light of the fact that] a man's ways are in full view of the LORD, and he examines all his paths."

Brothers, I am sure we would contentedly go along continually to lust—*slyly* when a live attractive woman is physically near to us, and *brazenly* when a woman is undressed or undressing on our motion picture, television, or computer screens—if no one were to know about it except ourselves, and we had *no fear* of any detrimental consequence.

That is not the case, thank God. Do we think we're the only ones doing the watching? Not so; for the Lord is watching also. Our ways are in "full view of the Lord." We are delighting in something we are viewing, and the Lord is *not in the least delighting* in what He is viewing—seeing us in our sin!

God said in Jeremiah 5:7-8, "I supplied all their needs, yet they committed adultery and thronged to the houses of prostitutes. They are well-fed, lusty stallions, *each neighing for another man's wife.*" There it is again—lusting after "another man's wife," the *exact same wording* as in our devotional today!

When we make imprudent choices in entertainment or simply do not look away, choose to turn it off completely, hit the skip button, or walk out of the room for a bit, we too have "thronged to the houses of prostitutes" of Jeremiah 5:7. The reality is we have been duped into consenting that the movie that is a hundred percent graphic sex scenes is X-rated or porn, but the R-rated movie with only a three-minute (soft porn) sex scene is acceptable entertainment and represents something *essential* to the plot line.

Unless he lives completely alone, a man with a daily Internet porn addiction, or even a *sporadic* dalliance problem, will nearly always cover his tracks. He'll erase his Web history and delete the "cookies." He'll attempt to remove and destroy "all his paths" he has traveled on.

Yet remember, Brothers, we have a loving, all-knowing, *all-seeing* God, and "he examines *all* his paths." A delete button hasn't been invented (and never will be) that can successfully obscure, remove, or destroy what God chooses to examine. "You have set our iniquities before you, our *secret sins* in the light of your presence" (Psalm 90:8).

That is why Solomon asked the rhetorical question, "Why embrace the bosom of another man's wife?" It is *rhetorical* in that he wasn't really asking a question to elicit any responses; he was saying, "Don't do it, Brothers!" "For a man's ways are in full view of the LORD."

---

1. In what figurative ways might a man "embrace the bosom of another man's wife"?

2. Does God see everything you do, even what you do "in secret"?

3. What is the relationship between Proverbs 5:20-21 and Psalm 90:8?

4. Are you trying to hide anything from God?

Day 30

"So I tell you this, and insist on it in the Lord, that you no longer live as the Gentiles do, in the futility of their thinking ... Having lost all sensitivity, they have given themselves over to sensuality so as to indulge in every kind of impurity, with a continual lust for more" (Ephesians 4:17 and 19).

It's only natural to romanticize how thrilling, courageous, and faithful the times and tenor of the first-century Church must have been. And had we solely the ardent adventures of the Book of Acts to capture the character and condition of the Church of that time, this lovely mental picture of ours would be wholly inarguable.

While their stories will always (and rightly so) inspire us and evoke great imagination and admiration, passages such as this one—centering on the Apostle Paul's reproof to the Ephesus believers—gives us another perspective; a sobering one, peering into a church made up of very *imperfect* lives. How uncanny, *how similar* people two thousand years ago were to us, so equally prone to regressing to the ways of *unenlightened unbelievers*—in this context termed "Gentiles."

What had happened to their faith in such a brief amount of time? What happened to their power and *resolve* that Paul had to implore them and in fact *insist* that they "no longer live as the Gentiles do"?

What has happened to *our* faith, Brothers? What happened to our resolve (memories of our lives *before* Christ) that the Holy Spirit must keep conducting His own course correction in our lives? Hadn't the Ephesian believers made up their minds *long* before this, once and for all, whom they were to going follow? And what about us? *Haven't we*?

The last thing any of us needs again is to be lost in the "futility" of our thinking. The problem is that when we become *desensitized* as they did—"having lost all sensitivity" (verse 19)—we do not comprehend how futile our thinking has become. Jesus was dismayed in Matthew 11:17 over the robotic, desensitized people surrounding Him: "We played the flute for you, and you did not dance; we sang a dirge, and you did not mourn." Once desensitized to the prickling and procession of God's Word and Spirit in our lives, we're vulnerable to "indulge in *every kind of impurity*, with a continual lust for more."

Our devotional today comes out of the fourth chapter to the church in Ephesus, which in its entirety is devoted to two things—first, promoting *unity, forbearance,* and *mutual service* in the Body of Christ (4:1-16); and, secondly, to tenets of holy, productive, *practical living* (4:17-32)—in everything from sensuality and purity matters (as we are discussing) to anger management and the kinds of words we choose. Tucked within these wise and practical instructions are some of the most alarming, arresting syllables you'll find anywhere in the entire sixty-six books of God's Holy

Library called the Bible. They are: "And do not *grieve* the Holy Spirit of God, with whom you were sealed for the day of redemption" (Ephesians 4:30).

It is nearly unfathomable that we can cause the Almighty pain! In the ultimate act, "the *full extent* of His love" (see metaphor in John 13:1-3), God chose to take upon himself the full force, fury, pain, and penalty of our sins on Calvary. "God made him who had no sin to be sin for us" (2 Corinthians 5:21). At that precise moment, when Christ and the Father were separated, Jesus cried out in anguish, "My God, my God, why hast thou forsaken me?" (Matthew 27:46, KJV).

For the first, only, and last time in all of history, the Father had turned His gaze away from the Son. His eyes were *too pure* to look upon the aggregate, undiluted sins of all humankind. Habakkuk 1:13 says "Your eyes are too pure to look on evil." Accordingly, God received unto himself the harshest and most *undeserved* suffering possible.

But here, in the context of *how we are to conduct our daily lives*, Paul said, "And do not grieve the Holy Spirit of God." The word "grieve" is about the strongest word possible to describe causing God pain. The only stronger choices (such as "terrorize" or "torture") are words that involve control over another, and no one and no thing can ever subdue and control God.

Brothers, each one of us *fervently* loves God. We want to *delight* Him. So let us be mindful of this exhortation when we are tempted to sin regarding any and "every kind of impurity," and let us no longer live as the unenlightened do. Let us retain (and where necessary, *regain*) our tactile sensitivity to the things of the Lord; let us never more give (deliver) ourselves over to sensuality; and let us *not ever, ever* grieve the Holy Spirit.

---

1. How, according to Paul, did the Gentiles of his day live? Are these characteristics comparable to the lives of people today?

2. How is your faith-level today?

3. How can you avoid being gradually desensitized by the immoral trends of our times?

4. In what ways do people grieve the Holy Spirit?

DAY 31

"Above all else, guard your heart, for it is the wellspring of life" (Proverbs 4:23).

The prepositional phrase "above all" appears sixteen times in the Bible, but the phrase "above all else" does not appear anywhere else in the Bible except here in Proverbs 4:23. I think it's safe to say then that what follows is more than a little bit important.

No one would have been in the least surprised if God's Word had said: Above all else love one another! Or, above all else pray without ceasing! Or, surely, above all else have faith in God! Instead God said: "Above all else, *guard your heart, for it is the wellspring of life.*"

The heart is the "wellspring of life" because it is the seat and center and sustenance of who *we've been*, who *we are*, and who we *are to become*. Most important, it is where Christ Jesus himself astoundingly takes up residence—there in the *believing* heart (see Ephesians 3:17). And it is where God's love dwells in us by faith: "God has poured out his love *into our hearts* by the Holy Spirit" (Romans 5:5).

For years I have wondered why it was Jesus in Luke 5:22 who—*reading their minds*—asked the Pharisees, "Why are you thinking these things *in your hearts?*" Everyone knows our minds, our brains, conduct thought. Right? So why didn't Jesus pose His question: "Why are you thinking these things in your *minds*?"

Elsewhere (in Matthew 15:19), Jesus did it again, teaching His disciples that "out of *the heart* [versus emanating out of the *mind*] come evil *thoughts*." Evidently, His disciple Peter retained this well, for later on he rebuked Simon the Sorcerer for such a wicked "*thought*" in his *"heart*" (see Acts 8:22).

Our minds are like computer storage devices and computer processors in the sense that they *enable* thinking (computing, so to speak), but the source and sustenance to our thinking is not in an organ at all, but resides in that mystery-hidden nether place the Bible refers to as our "hearts."

Consequently, we need to protect the spiritual integrity of our hearts more than a SWAT team shields their physical heart organs with protective body armor. We need to be wiser (in our hearts) at avoiding temptations. "A prudent man sees danger and takes refuge, but the simple *keep going* and suffer for it" (Proverbs 22:3).

Brothers, I implore you not to *keep going* in any areas you've been compromising in pertaining to male mental moral purity. *You don't want to suffer for it!* "In the paths of the wicked lie thorns and snares, but he who *guards his soul* stays far from them" (Proverbs 22:5).

The Holy Spirit is there for us to *help us* guard our hearts. Let's not disqualify ourselves then from His help because we're holding onto "eye candy," *clinging* onto worldliness! "Those who cling to worthless idols *forfeit the grace* that could be theirs" (Jonah 2:8). "Don't you know that friendship with the world is hatred toward God? Anyone who chooses to be a friend of the world becomes an enemy of God" (James 4:4).

Instead, Brothers, "Let us throw off everything that hinders and the sin that so easily entangles, and let us run with perseverance the race marked out for us, *fixing our eyes on Jesus*" (Hebrews 12:1-2).

Pornographic temptation is a danger, a snare, and a worthless idol all balled up in one. Were I to fall prey to this danger and snare—this spiritual *Kryptonite*—my spiritual life would be usurped of its highest fulfillment and my life in its entirety deprived of God's highest purposes for me.

My greatest fear is that at the end of my life, when my "flesh and body are spent," I would in pained agony of my soul mourn, "How I hated discipline! How *my heart* spurned correction! I would not obey my teachers or listen to my instructors. I have come to the brink of utter ruin in the midst of the whole assembly" (Proverbs 5:11-14).

I cannot—*will not*—let that happen. No, "The LORD *will fulfill his purpose for me*" (Psalm 138:8). I intend, with God's help, to *guard my heart*—to die at complete peace in anticipation of the joy of hearing: "Well done, good and faithful servant!… Come and share your master's happiness!" (Matthew 25:21). Won't you join me?

---

1. What is the wellspring of life?

2. Why should you guard your heart? How can you do so?

3. What must you do in order to avoid the thorns and snares of life?

4. What should your focal point be as you run life's race with perseverance?

5. What is the result of clinging to "worthless idols"?

6. What, according to the author, is "spiritual Kryptonite"?

7. What is God's purpose for your life?